# Leroy Thompson

# *Uniforms of the Soldiers of Fortune*

Illustrated by
Ken MacSwan

BLANDFORD PRESS
Poole · Dorset

First published in the UK 1985 by Blandford Press,
Link House, West Street, Poole, Dorset BH15 1LL

Copyright © 1985 Leroy Thompson

Distributed in the United States by
Sterling Publishing Co., Inc.,
2 Park Avenue, New York, NY 10016

ISBN 0 7137 1328 3

**British Library Cataloguing in Publication Data**

Thompson, Leroy
  Uniforms of the soldiers of fortune.
  1. Mercenary troops—History—Pictorial
  works   2. Uniforms, Military—History
  —Pictorial works
  I. Title
  355.3'5            UB321

Photoset in Monophoto Apollo
by August Filmsetting, Haydock, St Helens
and printed by Graficromo, Spain

# Contents

# Soldiers of Fortune Throughout History

Before beginning to trace the rather complex place the soldier of fortune holds in the history of warfare certain terms should be defined. 'Soldiers of fortune' has been chosen as the basis for this book rather than 'mercenaries' because it is a more comprehensive generic term. As normally defined, the mercenary fights for virtually any master who will pay his wages, though ideology may at least play some part in his choice of employers. The soldier of fortune, however, may fight for a country other than his own for many reasons, only one of which might be money. The soldier of fortune may serve a country he is drawn to ethnically, ideologically, religiously, or philosophically. He may also fight for another country because his own has been occupied or defeated by a foreign power, and he wants to continue fighting. Some may fight for a country other than their own to serve their own country's interests. Many fight just because they are drawn to the profession of arms, and they go to wherever there is a war. Throughout history the various foreign legions have been filled with such professional belliphiles. For that matter, the word 'soldier' stems from the medieval word 'solidarious' meaning a man serving for pay or, in simple terms, a mercenary. In this work 'soldier of fortune' has been used in the broadest context to allow for a wide and diverse coverage.

In antiquity, many soldiers of fortune were purely and simply mercenaries who fought for pay – often in the form of booty or plunder. The ancient Egyptians, for example, hired mercenary soldiers as early as 3000 BC; these ancient Egyptian mercenaries included Nubians, Asiatics, Libyans, and the Sea Peoples. Even the Hittites, among the most formidable professional warriors in history, used mercenaries to form much of their infantry. The army of ancient Israel also included mercenaries drawn from among others the Philistines.

Historically, the mercenary soldier is a member of a more militarily sophisticated society who sells his advanced skills to a more primitive army or a member of a barbaric society who sells his ferocity to a more sophisticated army. Frequently, such a soldier's skills are with some specialized weapon alien to the military system which employs him. One of the earliest examples of such a soldier for hire is the Greek hoplite. These heavily armed infantrymen with their long spears and well-ordered phalanx were the most formidable soldiers of their time and fought as mercenaries during the Greek and Persian Wars and during the Macedonian Wars. Under Darius, the Persian army contained up to 25 per cent mercenary hoplites in its infantry. In fact, the Greek mercenaries provided the Persians' staunchest opposition to Alexander. Other mercenary heavy infantry during the Greek and Persian Wars was provided by the Phrygians.

Since the Greeks specialized in the use of the sword and the spear, they normally had to hire most of their missile troops, thus providing a good market for mercenary slingers and archers in the Hellenic world. Cretan and Scythian archers, for example, were widely employed; the Cretans particularly being trained from childhood as soldiers for hire. Slingers from Rhodes and Thrace were also hired as mercenaries by Greek city states and by Alexander. Among other mercenary light infantrymen employed in ancient Greece was the peltast who specialized in the use of the javelin. The Greeks, being primarily heavy infantrymen, also provided employment opportunities to cavalrymen for hire such as the Thessalians.

During the Punic Wars the Carthaginians' great general Hannibal invaded Italy and stayed for 15 years with an army composed almost entirely of mercenaries. Though fighting for his own country, Hannibal must rank as one of the greatest 'mercenary captains' in history because of the great loyalty he inspired in the heterogeneous bunch of professionals who served him.

Perhaps the most important mercenary component of Hannibal's army was his Numidian light cavalry, whose change of employers to the Romans helped eventually spell Carthage's doom. Heavier Gallic and Spanish cavalrymen were also hired by Carthage to serve under Hannibal. Virtually all of Hannibal's infantry was composed of mercenaries, primarily from Spain, Gaul, and Libya. As were the Numidians, the Spaniards and Gauls were later hired by Rome to fight against their old employer Carthage. Other than javelinmen, Hannibal's armies were usually short of missile troops. The highly proficient mercenary slingers from the Balearic Islands provided him with the most effective troops of this class.

Though they hired mercenary troops away from the Carthaginians, the Romans did not really begin to make great use of mercenaries until the first century AD. Though the Republic had made limited use of mercenaries, the Roman Empire proved a great employer of soldiers for hire.

Once again as with the Greeks, the Romans were basically infantrymen; hence, many of their hired auxiliaries were missile troops, light infantry skirmishers, or cavalry. Many mercenary archers were Asiatics, but some Cretans still found employment with the Romans as did some of the Balearic slingers. Light infantrymen from Germany, Britain, and Spain were hired as skirmishers, while various types of 'barbarian' mercenary cavalrymen served at one time or another – Moors and Gauls being among the most frequently hired.

In Imperial Rome, the emperor eventually felt that a bodyguard composed of mercenaries would prove more loyal to the person of the sovereign and thus the Praetorian Guard came to be composed primarily of Germans and Britons.

In the Eastern Roman Empire (Byzantium) mercenaries formed a relatively minor part of the army in the earliest times but predominated by the early Middle Ages. Byzantine light cavalrymen – especially the Huns and Moors – were normally mercenaries, and the Varangian Guard which protected the Byzantine emperors was one of the most famous mercenary units in history, being drawn primarily from Vikings or Britons of Viking descent and at times containing within its ranks Nordic princes.

During the 'Dark Ages' and on through the Middle Ages and into the Renaissance, the difficulties in keeping a feudal levy in the field for any length of time and the constant warfare created an atmosphere in which free-lance (a term which originated to describe the knights for hire) soldiers flourished. During the period after the fall of the Western Roman Empire, Byzantium began to hire mercenary troops in far greater numbers since citizens could avoid military service by paying an exemption tax which was used to hire 'auxiliaries'. Among the mercenaries hired by the Byzantines between the Sixth and eleventh centuries were the Avars, Khazars, Saracens, Persians, Georgians, Armenians, Goths, and Huns. These free lances were normally used as light cavalry to support the Byzantine cataphracti and heavy infantry, though mercenary infantry was also used. Generally, the mercenaries fighting for the Byzantines proved loyal (i.e. They stayed bought.), but on a couple of notable occasions, the desertion of mercenary troops caused Byzantine defeats.

Some of Byzantium's enemies also used mercenary soldiers against the Eastern Empire. In the early seventh century, for example, the Lombards hired Avars as mercenaries against the Byzantines. During the tenth and eleventh centuries Magyars, Normans, and Germans also were hired by the Lombards. During the ninth and tenth centuries, the Franks hired Viking mercenaries to fight against other Vikings.

Between the tenth and twelfth centuries, the Russians hired Pechenegs, Khazars, Poles, Magyars, and Turks as mercenaries, who were paid for with a special tax. Even the famous Arab armies of the seventh through tenth centuries contained large numbers of mercenaries, known as 'Ghulams', who were purchased as slaves but who fought as mercenaries. Among those serving the Arabs as Ghulams were the Turks, Nubians, Berbers, Kurds, Slavs, Byzantines, Georgians, and Armenians. Some Rus also served the Arabs as mercenaries but were apparently free rather than slaves. These slave/mercenaries were the precursors of the Mamluks.

In England the Saxons hired Welshmen and Vikings as mercenaries. The most famous of the latter were probably the Huscarls who formed the bodyguard of the Saxon kings. The Saxons were, of course, defeated in 1066 by the Normans, who themselves had a long history as mercenaries. Normans had fought for various masters in Southern Italy and also against the Byzantines. When William the Conqueror invaded England, he took with him soldiers of fortune from all over Europe – French, Italian, and even Saracen mercenaries serving with the invaders.

In feudal Europe the practice of scutage, in which money could be paid to one's overlord in lieu of military service brought about an increased use of mercenaries. Mercenary knights – 'free lances' or 'knights errant' – found ready employment from the eleventh through the fourteenth centuries. Though knights from any country might be found seeking employment as mercenaries; Flemish, French, Breton, Burgundian, Gascon, or German knights were the most commonly encountered free lances.

As had been true historically, skilled missile troops, especially crossbowmen, were also high on the shopping list for any general seeking mercenary troops. In the thirteenth century, the Italians, Gascons, and Catalans were the premier crossbowmen and were widely hired by feudal generals, while later in the fourteenth century during the Hundred Years War, the French made wide use of Genoese and Spanish mercenary crossbowmen.

Mercenary infantry also saw relatively wide use during this time period with Flemish, Italian, Aragonese, Navarrese, and Basque being hired most often, especially by France. Despite the Lateran Edict late in the twelfth century against the use of mercenaries, the profession prospered, and permanent bands of mercenaries following one captain began to appear by the thirteenth century, thus sowing the seeds for the Golden Age of mercenary companies in the late Middle Ages and early Renaissance. Among the well-known mercenary captains of this period were William of Ypres, Mercadier, Cadoc, and Fawkes de Bréauté. Through the twelfth and thirteenth centuries unemployed mercenaries became a problem as they roamed the countryside of Europe looking for plunder or employment. 'Ribauds' or 'Brigands' (as they were also known) was a somewhat generic term for these unruly mercenary bands. By the late thirteenth century, true mercenary companies began to appear, the Grand Catalan Company being perhaps the best known.

By the thirteenth century the longbow had begun to be feared as the most devastating infantry weapon of its time in the hands of English and Welsh archers. Though originally Welsh longbowmen had been hired by Edward I as mercenaries, English longbowmen also saw some mercenary employment.

The importance of mercenaries in France has already been mentioned, but some idea of the wide use of such troops can be gained from an analysis of the more than 3000 mercenaries employed by Philip Augustus in 1202. Of this number, 524 were composed of knights or mounted sergeants (highly trained professional soldiers who normally were not of noble birth and ranked below knights in the feudal hierarchy, though they also fought as heavy cavalry), 219 of crossbowmen – both mounted and unmounted, and the remainder of infantry. The English kings also continued the wide use of mercenaries, though by the twelfth century the English hired mercenaries primarily for service in continental conflicts rather than for service in England.

During the thirteenth and fourteenth centuries, Spain made great use of Moslem mercenaries, especially Berber light cavalrymen. Christian mercenaries also continued to serve in Moslem armies during the twelfth, thirteenth, and fourteenth centuries. Castilians seem to have been the most numerous of these Christian free lances, though Portuguese and other nationalities also served.

During the twelfth and thirteenth centuries, Italy began the use of mercenary troops which would grow to mammoth proportions a few centuries later during the age of the Condotierri. The basis for the large mercenary armies which would appear later in Italy was laid in the middle of the thirteenth century with the establishment of the Tallia system whereby towns which were members of a league or alliance would pay to hire an entire company of mercenary troops to protect them. The Papal State also made use of mercenaries, particularly Normans, Lombards, and Tuscans, who could, of course, justify their pay by saying they were serving the church. Because of concentration on her fleet, Venice also proved a ready employer of mercenaries to fight her land battles and to serve as marines.

After the Norman conquest of Sicily late in the eleventh century and the establishment of the Kingdom of Sicily, the hiring of mercenaries became common on this island. Saracens and Berbers were hired by some Sicilian kings to form their personal bodyguards, while by the thirteenth century German mercenaries were widely employed.

In Russia, Turks or Kazaks were hired as mercenaries during the twelfth and thirteenth centuries, while Hungarian, Polish, German, and Lithuanian mercenaries – in many cases knights – were also hired in some parts of Russia.

The Crusades and particularly the Crusader states established as enclaves in the East by the Crusaders also generated employment for mercenaries. Western knights were hired by the Crusader states as mercenaries; often these mercenaries were Crusaders who decided to stay in the east for pay. Mercenary light cavalry and infantry, however, were hired from among eastern Christians such as the Syrians, Armenians, and Maronites. Of the Syrians the most numerous were the Turcopoles, who were very effective light cavalrymen.

In a few cases westerners – 'Franks' as they were known –

fought as mercenaries in Moslem armies, particularly for the Sultans of Rum during the thirteenth century. These Franks were often former prisoners of other Moslems. There are also recorded cases of Frankish knights serving the Egyptians during the twelfth and thirteenth centuries.

After their defeat by the Seljuks at Manzikert in 1071, the Byzantines began to place a greater and greater reliance on mercenaries. In the late eleventh and early twelfth centuries, Byzantine armies might contain soldiers for hire from any of the following groups: Colbingians, Armenians, French, Germans, Flemings, Normans, Italians, English, Saracens, Russians, Rumanians, Norse, Cumans, Seljuks, Pechenegs, Uzes, Alans, Slavs, Bulgars, Serbs, and Georgians.

For the next two centuries, the Byzantines drew heavily on these sources of manpower for their armies. Certain ethnic and national groups predominated under different emperors, though Turks and 'Franks' normally predominated. The most famous mercenary band of the early fourteenth century, Roger de Flor's Grand Catalan Company, served Byzantium as well. De Flor is often considered the first of the Condotierri.

The later Medieval period offered perhaps the greatest market in history for the mercenary soldier as the Hundred Years War, the Burgundian Wars, and the Wars of the Roses created opportunities for trained soldiers.

Unemployed soldiers of fortune during the Hundred Years War began forming 'Free Companies' about the middle of the fourteenth century, often capturing a castle or two from which they could control an area and exact tribute. The captains of such companies were normally Englishmen or Gascons, and the soldiers were primarily English, Scots, Germans, Gascons, Spanish, or Navarrese. Reminiscent of the later French Foreign Legion, one such company was even known as the 'Compagnie des Batards' (company of bastards), a reference in part to the leaders, who were often illegitimate sons of noblemen, and in part to the motley nature of the troops. Among the more famous leaders of the Free Companies were such men as Bascot de Mauléon, Bertrand du Guesclin, Sir Robert Knollys, and

Werner von Ürslingen. Knollys' company, one of the largest, was comprised of between 600 and 1000 men, a large proportion archers. Though mercenary companies, the Free Companies were well organized, even having an officer in charge of sharing out booty according to a fixed schedule. Occasionally, many companies would band together for major operations such as the ones carried out in the Saône and Rhône valleys in the mid-fourteenth century by the Grand Company, composed of over 16,000 men. Occasionally, certain captains would rise to such prominence that they became, in effect, generals over many Free Companies. Sêguin de Badefol and Geoffrey Têtonoire were two such captains.

Although having many employers, the Free Companies served the King of Navarre and his French enemies perhaps most frequently. In 1366, the Black Prince also hired 12,000 companions. In Italy, Free Companies, which were forerunners of the later bands raised by the great Condottieri, appeared in great numbers by the mid-fourteenth century, with Germans being by far the most numerous of these companions. Among the companies operating in Italy during the second half of the fourteenth century were the Great Company, the White Company, the Breton Company, the Company of the Star, and the Company of the Rose. Among the most famous mercenary captains of the period were Sir John Cresswell and John Hawkwood, the latter the leader of the famed White Company, which by 1363 numbered nearly 5000 men, mostly English and divided about equally between men-at-arms and archers.

Near the end of the fourteenth century, the Company of St George was the last of the Free Companies in Italy, their places being taken by the companies in the employ of the Condottieri. The term 'condottieri' came from the contracts of employment – 'condotte' – between the mercenary captain and his employer – normally one of the Italian city states. Such contracts often were very detailed, and by the fifteenth century usually ran for periods of six months to a year. Some Condottieri were even paid a retainer when a state was not at war so that they would have their company ready for service should they be needed.

The Condottieri companies varied in size from less than 50 to more than 1000, with the smaller companies often being hired by a major Condottieri in order to fulfil the number of troops called for in his contract. During the first half of the fifteenth century, the Condottieri dominated warfare in Italy, and their ranks attracted soldiers of fortune from all over Italy, many captains rising to positions of great wealth and power. Among the more famous of the Condottieri families were Sforza, Attendolo, Colonna, Malatesta, Orsini, Sanseverino, and dal Verme.

One other important source of Italian mercenary soldiers was Genoa, whose excellent crossbowmen and sailors were hired by the French throughout the Hundred Years War. The Hundred Years War, in fact, saw both the English and the French — the latter far more predominantly — making use of mercenary troops, including free-lance artillerymen who were hired to handle the cannon which saw use at Agincourt and elsewhere.

Many Free Companies had seen action in Spain as well during the fourteenth century as they were hired to help press various claims to the throne of Castile. In some cases unemployed Free Companies entered Spain from France, primarily in search of new territory to pillage. Moslem mercenaries from North Africa were also hired by Castile during the fourteenth and fifteenth centuries.

One of the richest kingdoms of the latter Middle Ages was Burgundy, which made extensive use of mercenaries, especially Italians and Englishmen. Even some of the Condottieri were hired by Burgundy. During the late fifteenth century, however, the Burgundians were defeated at Grandson, Morat, and Nancy, thus heralding their decline as a military power.

By defeating the Burgundians, the Swiss pikemen, on the other hand, had established themselves along with the English bowmen as the most formidable fighting men of their time. So effective were the Swiss that they became the most sought after mercenaries in Europe by the end of the fifteenth century, with France being their principal employer. Because of their successes, the Swiss pikemen were soon emulated by the German Landsknechts who proved the Swiss's greatest rivals among fellow mercenaries during the fifteenth century.

In England during the fifteenth century, the Wars of the Roses and the constant shifting of loyalties which resulted made the hiring of mercenaries from the continent an attractive proposition, and German, Swiss, Burgundian, Flemish, and French mercenaries were hired at one time or another during the struggle for England's throne. In reality, the number of foreign mercenaries hired at any one time did not exceed 2000, but among those hired were handgunners such as the 300 Flemish hired by Charles the Bold to support the claim of Edward IV.

Scots soldiers of fortune had also begun a long-standing tradition of serving with the French in the fourteenth century, and by the late fifteenth century Scots mercenaries formed the personal bodyguard for the King of France.

In 1506, Pope Julius II formed the Swiss Guards, which have continued as the Papal guard until today. In 1527, 189 Swiss guards died to a man defending Pope Clement VII against other mercenaries from Spain and Germany. Not only the Vatican, but France and Austria would later incorporate units of Swiss mercenaries to serve as royal guards.

Although the Swiss and the German Landsknechts continued to be the dominant mercenary elements during the early sixteenth century, their pre-eminence on the battlefield was being eclipsed by the highly-trained Spanish tercios comprised of pikemen and arquebusiers. As a result well-trained Spanish troops became among the most sought-after mercenaries of the sixteenth century. Other Spaniards – the Conquistadores – were classic soldiers of fortune, conquering large portions of the New World for Spain. Cortez, who conquered Mexico, even made use of the Totonacs as mercenaries in defeating the Aztecs.

Some Spaniards became mercenaries for other reasons, such as the excellent engineer and commander Pedro Navarro who was captured by the French at Ravenna and entered their service when Spain failed to ransom him. He became one of France's foremost generals. Such foreign captains were not uncommon in France during this period. The victor at Seminara in 1495, Marshal Everard d'Aubigny, was actually a Scotsman – a member, in fact, of the Stewart family. Seminara, by the way, was the great Spanish general Cordoba's only defeat.

The reputation of mercenaries in the late fifteenth and early sixteenth centuries was not good. Most armies were composed primarily of mercenaries, yet their loyalty was always suspect. The Swiss were especially well-known for being difficult, and it was standard practice for mercenary units to demand bonuses on the eve of battle and to refuse to fight if the bonuses were not paid.

England still continued to hire mercenaries in the sixteenth century, Henry VIII using continental mercenaries to invade France from Calais in 1513. Englishmen and Scotsmen turned up as mercenaries rather frequently too. To name just a few instances, there were Englishmen as well as other mercenaries aiding the knights of St John in the defense of Malta in 1565, and there were Irish and Scots in the Spanish army under Parma in 1588. At the end of the sixteenth century English soldiers of fortune led by Anthony and Sir Robert Shirley helped reorganize and train the Persian army. Robert, an artillery expert, organized the Persian artillery which later proved very effective against the Turks.

The sixteenth century also began the great era of siegecraft which would culminate in the seventeenth century. As a result, mercenary siege engineers and free-lance master gunners, the latter mostly from France and Germany, were in great demand. Even such well-known 'engineers' as Leonardo da Vinci and Michelangelo sold their services as experts in siegecraft and fortifications.

The seventeenth century saw the beginnings of national armies which would portend the decline of large-scale use of mercenary forces, but not for many years would this transition be complete. Early in the new century the Spanish army, for example, still contained German, Scottish, Italian, English, Burgundian, and Walloon soldiers of fortune, and by 1621 the composition of Spanish mercenary contingents had changed only in that the English and Scots had been replaced by the Irish.

The Thirty Years War, which began in 1618, stimulated the hiring of mercenaries by many of the belligerents. In 1618, for example, mercenary leader Count Ernst Von Marsfeld captured Pilsen with 20,000 mercenaries. However, when payment was later delayed, Marsfeld led his men on an orgy of pillage in the Rhineland.

The Dutch and French were both great employers of mercenaries during the Thirty Years War, but even Gustavus Adolphus employed very high caliber Scottish mercenaries. English or Scottish soldiers of fortune, in fact, fought for the United Provinces, Sweden, and France during the conflict.

The Thirty Years War was also a profitable time for the mercenary entrepreneur who could furnish large armies ready to take the field. The greatest of these soldiers of 'fortune-making' was Wallenstein who recruited heavily during the 1620s and eventually had his own army of over 20,000 men equipped and supplied by him and ready to go into action.

Another highly successful soldier of fortune during the Thirty Years War was Duke Friedrich Hermann of Schomberg, who led the French army which halted an invading Spanish army on the French frontier in 1637.

During the English Civil War, the most famous soldier of fortune was probably Prince Rupert of the Rhine, who, though a great soldier, could not single-handedly defeat the Parliamentary army. Later, Rupert and other Royalists took service with European armies after leaving England. Royalist mercenaries from France also served under Montrose in Scotland at the Battle of Carbiesdale in 1650. English Jacobites also fought for Don Juan of Austria in 1658 at the Battle of the Dunes.

Later in the century in 1674, one of England's greatest soldiers — John Churchill, later the Duke of Marlborough — served as a soldier of fortune in the French army leading the

Royal English Regiment. Some experts believe the knowledge of French tactics gained at that time later helped Marlborough defeat his former employers.

The late seventeenth century also saw the formation within the French army of an Irish Brigade, beginning the long tradition of the 'Wild Geese' (a term which would eventually become synonymous with soldier of fortune) serving in the French army, most often against the hated English.

Throughout the eighteenth century, the Wild Geese continued to serve France and, in lesser numbers, Spain. The distinction of being the most ubiquitous mercenaries during the 1700s, however, probably belongs to the Germans, since the princes of various German principalities earned their incomes by hiring out their subjects as soldiers. As a result, Germans served with the English in Flanders at the beginning of the century, and troops from Brunswick, Hesse-Cassel, Waldeck, Anspach-Bayreuth, and Anhalt-Zerbst – to a total of 30,000 men – fought for England later in the century during the American Revolution.

Frederick the Great, himself the greatest German soldier of the century, even had to resort to hiring mercenaries to flesh out his infantry during the middle years of the century, though the 'Freibataillone und Freicorps' serving Frederick did not measure up to the highly professional standards of the Prussian army.

Maria Theresa also made extensive use of 'Free Companies', the most famous of which, the Panduren-Corps von der Trenck, acted as a relatively successful free-lance commando unit when not busy raping and pillaging.

American Indians were widely hired as mercenaries in the New World, too. During the French and Indian Wars both France and Britain made use of Indian irregulars, while Britain used Indians – especially the Iroquois – during the American Revolution.

The American Revolution also offered an opportunity for soldiers of fortune who believed in the American cause. Among the most famous of these men were three officers who contributed greatly to the American victory – Lafayette, von Steuben, and Kosciusko. When the French entered the war on the American side their forces also contained a predecessor of later French foreign legions in Lauzun's Legion which was composed of various continental soldiers of fortune. Hessians in turn were recruited from southern Germany by the British Army. After the Revolutionary War was won, the new republic's foremost naval hero – John Paul Jones – himself became a sailor of fortune and took service as a rear admiral in the Russian navy.

For the true soldier of fortune, however, India offered perhaps the best opportunity as the Moguls, early in the century, and various princes, later in the century, sought European officers to help modernize their armies. Portuguese, French, Dutch, English, Irish, Scottish, German, Italian, and Eurasian officers, among others, flocked to serve these Indian rulers. Among the most famous of these soldiers of fortune were de Boigne, Thomas, Perron, and Skinner.

Swiss mercenaries also continued to serve in various armies during the eighteenth century, though they were nowhere as prevalent nor as important as they had been a few centuries earlier. In 1792, the Swiss Guards serving Louis XVI were massacred when the Tuileries was stormed.

If earlier centuries had seen the mercenary in predominance, the nineteenth century saw the ascendance of the soldier of fortune who fought for another country not just for profit but for conviction and perhaps for adventure. The century would also see the formation of the two most famous modern 'mercenary' units – the French Foreign Legion and the Gurkha Rifles.

The King's German Legion, for example, consisted of Hanoverian troops who had fled to England after the French had occupied their country. In one sense the King's German Legion might be called mercenaries since they were being paid by a foreign power, but they were also fighting for their own ruler since the British king was the Elector of Hanover.

Irish 'Wild Geese' continued to serve France and Spain in

their own regiments during the early years of the nineteenth century, but by the end of the Napoleonic Wars the Irish regiments in both armies were no more. Although the Napoleonic Wars were fought primarily by national armies there were still soldiers of fortune who fought on each side. A few Americans, for example, served France at one time or another as did other 'revolutionaries'. On the other side, de Watteville's Regiment composed of Swiss, Germans, and other nationalities fought for Great Britain, being used for amphibious operations in the Mediterranean among other duties.

Great Britain also found herself fighting the United States, and at the Battle for New Orleans faced soldiers of fortune serving the USA in the persons of refugees from Santa Domingo and pirates from the Caribbean.

The return of the monarchy to France after the defeat of Napoleon at Waterloo also saw the return for a few years of Swiss regiments serving a French king, but by 1830 the use of Swiss mercenaries had stopped once again. In 1831, however, what remains today as one of the most famous bodies of soldiers of fortune in history was formed by France. In that year the French Foreign Legion came into existence, at least partially in an attempt to get the recently discharged Swiss and German mercenaries out of France. The new legionnaires were sent to North Africa to fight France's colonial wars. They were soon involved in the Carlist War in Spain (1834–39); later in the century, Legionnaires would fight in the Crimea (1854), Italy (1859), Mexico (where Camerone, one of the Legion's most famous battles, took place in 1863), and France itself during the Franco-Prussian War (1870). In addition to North Africa, Legionnaires saw colonial service in Tonkin, Dahomey, and Madagascar.

Even before the French Foreign Legion was formed, the British had accepted the first regiments of Gurkhas into the East India Company's army in 1815. Along with the Legion, the Gurkhas would establish a long tradition of loyalty despite being termed 'mercenaries'. Throughout the nineteenth century, Gurkha regiments fought in India and the Far East. For example, Gurkhas saw action in the Sikh Wars during the 1840s and the Indian Mutiny (during which they stayed loyal to the British) in the 1850s. Throughout the rest of the century, the Gurkhas were used all over India, but primarily along the Northwest frontier against the Afghans.

The East India Company also offered an excellent opportunity for British or other European soldiers of fortune wanting to serve as officers in India.

The first quarter of the nineteenth century saw revolutions against Spain and Portugal in South America, and many soldiers of fortune fought in these wars of independence. Englishmen, North Americans, Irishmen, and Germans predominated among those taking service in South America. Probably the best known among these adventurers was Lord Thomas Cochrane, a British sailor who commanded the Chilean navy. A true sailor of fortune, he also served at one time or another as an admiral in the Brazilian, Greek, and British navies.

Cochrane's service with the Greek navy was during the Greek War of Independence against Turkey. Many Englishmen – known as 'Philhellenes' – flocked to Greece's cause, Lord Byron perhaps being the most famous, though certainly not the most effective. Cochrane and General Sir George Church gave the most valuable assistance. At Navarino, the naval battle that ensured Greece's freedom from Turkey in 1827, at least one prominent French soldier of fortune – Letellier – was serving the Egyptians as well.

During the early 1840s Giuseppe Garibaldi, best remembered for his fight to unite Italy, served as a soldier of fortune in South America. Remaining an adventurer until the end of his life, Garibaldi later commanded a group of volunteers for France during the Franco-Prussian War. He was offered but declined a command in the Union Army in the Civil War. Garibaldi's cause in Italy attracted soldiers of fortune from other parts of Europe who joined his forces and helped him gain victory. Included were many Englishmen. The Garibaldinis continued after their founder's death finally seeing service in the French army in World War I.

In the USA, during the Mexican war, the Americans hired a 'Spy Company' composed of Mexican bandits and some North Americans who served as scouts. In fact, the hiring of irregulars as scouts has been one of the primary uses of mercenaries or adventurers in the US armed forces. For example, Indian scouts hired to track other tribes were widely used during the Indian Wars of the latter half of the nineteenth century.

In the Crimean War, soldiers of fortune still turned up as well. The French Foreign Legion's service has already been mentioned. One of the foremost Turkish generals, Omar Pasha, was also a Croat soldier of fortune whose real name was Michael Lattas. While the Crimean War was still going on, in Central America an American soldier of fortune named William Walker with a force of 56 men was taking over Nicaragua. He later tried to take over Honduras as well but was unsuccessful and was tried and executed.

The American Civil War during the 1860s offered an opportunity for soldiers of fortune, who fought for both sides, though the Confederacy seems to have attracted more than the Union. Henry Stanley of 'Doctor Livingstone I presume' fame had the distinction of fighting on both the Union and Confederate sides; another prominent English soldier of fortune serving the Confederacy was Col. George St Leger Grenfell.

After the defeat of the Confederacy, many former members of the Southern army left the South to take service with foreign armies, some going to Mexico and some taking service as far away as Africa and the Far East.

The latter part of the nineteenth century was a fertile period for colonial warfare and offered opportunities for soldiers of fortune to fight in 'far off places with strange-sounding names'. It was also a period when European and American 'advisors' were hired by some of the less advanced countries to assist in modernizing their armies. It was a time of individual soldiers of fortune, however, rather than 'free companies'. Only the

French Foreign Legion remained for those wishing to join an institutionalized group of soldiers of fortune.

During the twentieth century the French Foreign Legion and the Gurkhas remained the foremost inheritors of the traditions of the old Free Companies. The early years of the century saw many opportunities for soldiers of fortune – especially from the USA – in Mexico fighting for or against Zapata or Villa or in other parts of Latin America. The Far East, especially China, was also a fertile ground for soldiers of fortune who were hired to lead and train the armies of feudal warlords.

Although World War I was primarily fought by large national armies, there were still a few opportunities for soldiers of fortune. Both the French Foreign Legion and British Gurkha regiments fought in World War I. In Arabia, T.E. Lawrence established himself as one of the archetypal soldiers of fortune of history as he led an Arab revolt against the Turks. Many Americans also managed to see action before the USA's entrance into the war. Some joined the French Foreign Legion while others posed as Canadians and joined the British Army. The most famous group of American soldiers of fortune in World War I, however, remains the aviators of the Escadrille Lafayette.

American flyers, in fact, established a tradition of searching for action in other lands. In 1920, for example, Americans traveled to Poland to form the Kosciusko Squadron which flew against the Russians in the Russo-Polish War. Other American aviators turned up in the fledgling air forces of Latin American and African countries.

Shortly after World War I ended – in 1920 to be exact – another important haven for soldiers of fortune was created in the Spanish Foreign Legion, though unlike the French Foreign Legion, the Spanish Legion has not relied primarily upon foreigners. Still, though Spaniards predominated in its ranks, the Spanish Foreign Legion has attracted its share of foreign soldiers of fortune over the years. It should be noted, by the way, that Frenchmen were not allowed to join, though more than one did by claiming to be Belgian or Swiss.

British soldiers of fortune – including such men as F.G. Peake and John Glubb – found a home during the 1920s and 30s in the Jordanian Arab Legion which had carried on the traditions of Lawrence's Arab Army. British officers, in fact, found service all over the Middle East, but the Arab Legion always seemed to be the most romantic source of employment.

Between 1932 and 1935 the Gran Chaco War between Bolivia and Paraguay was fought by two armies officered and trained by foreign soldiers of fortune. Germans, Czechs, and Spaniards provided officers for the Bolivians, while Frenchmen, Britons, and White Russians supplied officers for the Paraguayans.

The Spanish Civil War, which began in 1936, also offered wide scope for foreign adventurers and zealots. In addition to the professionals of the Spanish Foreign Legion who fought on the Nationalist side, the German Condor Legion and Italian Volunteer Corps served as 'volunteers' with their fellow Fascists. Sympathizers from many parts of the world also joined the Republican forces. Russians provided a large foreign contingent, while Americans formed the Abraham Lincoln Battalion (later a brigade). There were also large contingents of British and French, who fought for the Republicans. Individuals from other countries fought for the Nationalists and the Republicans, depending on whether their political leanings were to the right or left. Sympathizers with the Nationalists were normally required to join the Spanish Foreign Legion to serve.

World War II was once again primarily a war fought by large national armies, though there were plenty of opportunities for the soldier of fortune. The French Foreign Legion fought the Germans early in the war. After the fall of France, the 13th DBLE continued the fight as part of the Free French, while other Legion units, which had remained loyal to the Vichy regime, re-entered the conflict after the allied victory in North Africa. The Gurkhas are remembered especially for their great fighting qualities in the Western Desert, Italy and in Burma; Nepalese recruits flocked to the standard so that Gurkha strength was greatly increased during the war.

Once again American aviators could not wait to enter the fighting. Some went to fly in China as part of the American Volunteer Group (often known as 'The Flying Tigers'), while others served Great Britain as members of the RAF's Eagle Squadron. Germany also had volunteers who served her. Some were drawn from conquered countries and served as contingents in the Waffen SS, while others such as the Free Indian Legion were drawn from POWs. The Spanish Blue Division, on the other hand, was comprised of Spanish Fascists who volunteered to fight Communism in Russia. In Burma, the American OSS also made good use of tribal irregulars in the Kachin and Jinghpaw Rangers.

After their defeat in World War II, many German professional soldiers took service in the French and Spanish Foreign Legions. By the late 1940s many of these same Germans were fighting and dying for their old enemy France in Indochina. Other Germans found service in the Middle East training the armies of some of the newly independent Moslem states. Many of these German-trained armies would be in action in 1948 against the new state of Israel. Israel, itself, drew on Jewish – and in a few cases gentile – soldiers of fortune who served the army of the new state from religious or moral conviction. One of these – Mickey Marcus – was an American staff officer who performed much the same type of service for Israel that von Steuben had performed for the new American state.

The post-World War II years also saw at least two well-known special forces officers of wartime fame – David Stirling of the Special Air Service and Otto Skorzeny of the Jagdverbände – emerge as entrepreneurs and recruiters of mercenaries. In both cases, however, it is hard to pigeon-hole these men as modern 'Condottieri'. Stirling, for example, seemed to retain many ties with the British government. Skorzeny's endeavors, on the other hand, seemed to be linked with the interests of ODESSA, an organization of former SS men.

During the Korean War, there were few soldiers of fortune on the allied side, though from the Communist point of view,

29

the Chinese 'volunteers' might be called soldiers of fortune who were fighting from conviction.

During the 1960s and 1970s, British officers continued to serve in the Middle East, especially in Oman where the Trucial Oman Scouts and the Sultan's army were officered by Britons. American and other soldiers of fortune – including Che Guevara who was actually an Argentinian – served with Castro during the Cuban Revolution in the late 1950s.

The 1960s also saw the re-emergence in Africa of the mercenary in the traditional sense. In the Congo and Biafra, mercenary companies led by such men as Mike Hoare, Bob Denard, Jean Schramme, and Rolf Steiner saw wide use as shock troops against poorly trained African troops. The Sudan, Yemen, and, later, Angola would also see the employment of mercenary units.

In Vietnam the USA made use of mercenaries despite denials to the contrary. In fact, at one point negotiations were being carried out with Great Britain and Nepal to hire the Gurkhas to serve in Vietnam. The best of the US employed local 'mercenaries' were the Nungs and the Montagnards in Vietnam and Vang Pao's Meos in Laos. It has been reported that the US also hired at least a small number of European soldiers of fortune for certain special missions. Air America offered employment opportunities for a large number of 'free-lance' flyers willing to transport, 'Anything, Anywhere, Anytime.' On the other side, the NVA and VC had occasional European 'volunteers' recruited from Warsaw Pact countries, deserters from the French Foreign Legion during the Indochina War, and American turncoats. Though few in numbers, these 'volunteers' may have been by the definition used in this work 'soldiers of fortune'.

The disillusionment felt by many American veterans of Vietnam and the urge to continue to fight Communism offered the perfect breeding ground for soldiers of fortune. As a result, many Americans ended up fighting for Southern Rhodesia. Others served and are still serving with the South African armed forces. Still others took service in Latin America, the traditional place of employment for North American adventurers. The Angolan Civil War and the continuing conflict in that country also attracted some Americans, though Portuguese soldiers of fortune have seen the most action there.

During the 1980s and as this book is being written, soldiers of fortune continue to find employment. El Salvador, Guatemala, and other Latin American armies, for example, are using American soldiers of fortune as advisors. Americans and Europeans also serve with various factions in the civil war which rages constantly in Lebanon, while Moslems from all over the world serve as soldiers of fortune with PLO forces. Moammar Khadafy has even recruited his own 'Moslem Legion' from various sources. Many of the armies of the Persian Gulf states make use of their oil wealth to recruit foreign 'advisors', officers, and NCOs. British officers are still hired, and a large number of Pakistanis take service with Gulf states armies.

In almost a throwback to the Middle Ages, the last few years have seen virtually a return to the feudal use of free companies as mercenary leaders have attempted to seize control of tiny third world countries. This happened first with Bob Denard's 1978 operation in the Comoros and more recently with Mike Hoare's unsuccessful attempt to seize the Seychelles in 1981.

In fact, the weapons have changed and the numbers of men involved have changed; it is questionable, however, if the motivation has changed all that much between the free-lance soldiers of 500 years ago and of today. Admittedly, there was far more potential for profit as a free-lance during the Renaissance. Still, most free-lance soldiers have historically chosen the profession of arms either because they preferred conflict to status or because they felt there was something worth fighting for, even if their lawful government did not. Things have not changed that much today. Many free-lance soldiers are professional combat troops, not professional peacetime soldiers. Many — especially those fighting against Communist insurgencies — feel they are fighting the fight their governments should be fighting. If anything, today's soldier of fortune is far more altruistic than his predecessor, but he still chooses adventure over security.

**Plate 1** ANCIENT

1. Sherden

2. Numidian Light Cavalryman

3. Greek Mercenary Hoplite

**Plate 2** ANCIENT

4. Cretan Archer

5. Balearic Slinger

6. Levantine Archer

**Plate 3** DARK AGES/MIDDLE AGES

7. Ribaud

8. Hun

9. Varangian

**Plate 4** MIDDLE AGES

10. Genoese Crossbowman

11. Landsknecht

12. Swiss Pikeman

**Plate 5** MIDDLE AGES/RENAISSANCE

13. Welsh Mercenary Archer

14. Companion
Man-at-Arms
of the White Company

15. Papal Swiss Guardsman

**Plate 6** MIDDLE AGES/RENAISSANCE

17. Condottieri

16. Mercenary Artillerist

18. Grand Catalan Companion
(Almulgavar)

**Plate 7** 18th/19th CENTURIES

19. Scots Guardsman,
France (c. 1700)

20. Private,
Regiment Lally
(c. 1760)

21. Private,
Regiment Irlanda
(c. 1805)

# Plate 8  18th/19th CENTURIES

22. Swiss Guardsman,
France
(c. 1740)

23. Panduren
von der Trenck

24. Dragoon,
Schwarze Brigade
Favrat

**Plate 9** 18th/19th CENTURIES

25. King's
German Legionnaire

26. Ninja

27. Swiss Guardsman,
Austria (c. 1745)

**Plate 10** AMERICAN REVOLUTION

28. Major General
Friedrich von Steuben

29. Hesse-Cassel
Jaeger

30. Hussar,
Lauzun's Legion

**Plate 11** 18th/19th CENTURIES

31. General de Brigada
Lee Christmas

32. Major,
Madras Engineers
(c. 1840)

33. Philhellene

**Plate 12** GURKHAS

35. Gurkha Rifleman,
World War I

34. Rifleman,
2nd Gurkha Rifles
(late 19th Century)

36. Subadar-Major,
3rd Gurkha Rifles
(c. 1905)

**Plate 13** FRENCH FOREIGN LEGION

7. Legionnaire, RMLE,
World War I

38 Caporal,
Solferino, 1859

39 Caporal chef,
3rd REI,
Morocco (1930s)

**Plate 14** 20th CENTURY

40. T.E. Lawrence

41. Lieutenant General
John Glubb

42. Tracy Richardson

**Plate 15** 1920s–30s

43. Major General
Frank 'One Arm'
Sutton

44. Major,
Bolivian Army
(Chaco War)

45. Frank Tinker
(Spanish Civil War)

**Plate 16** SPANISH FOREIGN LEGION

46. Legionnaire
    1st Class
    (Spanish Civil War)

47. Corporal
    (early 1930s)

48. Lieutenant
    (early 1920s)

**Plate 17** SPANISH CIVIL WAR

49. Lieutenant,
    Condor Legion

50. Machine-Gunner,
    Abraham Lincoln Battalion

51. Tanker,
    Italian Volunteer

**Plate 18** AVIATORS OF FORTUNE

52. 1st Lieutenant,
Kosiuszko Squadron

53. 2nd Lieutenant,
Escadrille Lafayette

54. Flying Officer, RAF
Eagle Squadron

**Plate 19** WORLD WAR II GERMAN VOLUNTEERS

55. Lieutenant,
    Spanish 'Blue Division',
    Russia

56. Sturmann,
    13th Waffen-Gibirgs-Division
    der SS 'Handschar'

57. Free India Legionnaire

**Plate 20** FLYING TIGERS

58. Flying Tiger

59. Flying Tiger

60. Flying Tiger

**Plate 21** FRENCH FOREIGN LEGION

61. Legionnaire,
3rd REI, Algeria
(c. 1951)

63. Caporal,
13th DBLE,
Bir Hakeim,
World War II

62. Sergent-chef,
1st BEP, Indochina
(c. 1951)

**Plate 22** GURKHAS

64. Gurkha Rifleman,
Malaya (c. 1957)

65. Gurkha Rifleman,
4th Indian Division,
World War II

66. Rifleman,
2/7th Duke of Edinburgh's
Own Gurkha Rifles,
Hong Kong (1982)

**Plate 23** VIETNAM

67. Nung,
SOG Recon Team
(c. 1970)

68. Montagnard 'Striker'
(c. 1965)

69. Air America Pilot

**Plate 24** SPANISH FOREIGN LEGION

70. Lieutenant (c. 1965)

71. Legionnaire,
Sahara (c. 1975)

72. Gastadore, VI Bandara
(c. 1950)

**Plate 25** MERCENARY LEADERS, AFRICA

73. Major Mike Hoare

74. 'Colonel' Bob Denard

75. 'Colonel' Rolf Steiner

**Plate 26** MIDDLE EAST

76. Captain,
Trucial Oman Scouts
(c. 1965)

77. David Smiley,
the Yemen (1960s)

78. Islamic 'Volunteer',
PLO Main Force,
Lebanon (1983)

**Plate 27** AFRICA

79. William Baldwin,
    Kenya (1954)

80. Bushman, 201 Battalion,
    Southwest African
    Territorial Force (1983)

81. Major Mike Williams,
    Grey's Scouts,
    Rhodesia (1977)

**Plate 28** AMERICAN SOLDIERS OF FORTUNE

82. Robert K. Brown

83. Mike Echanis

84. Mickey Marcus

**Plate 29** SPANISH FOREIGN LEGION

85. Legionnaire
of Special Operations
Unit (c. 1978)

87. Legionnaire,
Sahara (c. 1975)

86. Corporal, Armored Cavalry,
'Grupos Ligeros Saharianos II
(c. 1976)

**Plate 30** RECENT SOLDIERS OF FORTUNE

88. Portuguese Mercenary,
Angola

89. Swiss Guardsman,
Vatican (current)

90. American 'Advisor',
Guatemala

**Plate 31** FRENCH FOREIGN LEGION

91. Caporal,
1st REC (c. 1978)

92. Caporal, 2nd Cie,
2nd REP (c. 1983)

93. Legionnaire,
13th DBLE,
Djibouti (c. 1977)

**Plate 32** GURKHAS

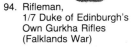

94. Rifleman,
    1/7 Duke of Edinburgh's
    Own Gurkha Rifles
    (Falklands War)

95. Piper,
    7th Duke of Edinburgh's
    Own Gurkha Rifles
    (c. 1971)

96. Sergeant Rambahadur Limbu VC
    10th Princess Mary's
    Own Gurkha Rifles

# Colour Plate Descriptions

## 1 Sherden

The Sherdens were one of the 'Sea Peoples' and seem to have originally visited Egypt as pirates. They were excellent warriors, however, and many of them were recruited as mercenaries by Rameses II. In addition to serving as the Pharoah's personal bodyguard, the Sherdens came to be considered among the best troops in the Egyptian army. They fought with distinction at Kadesh in 1288 BC against the Hittites, helping to defend Rameses until reinforcements arrived when he was surrounded early in the battle by the enemy. Though many Sherdens served Egypt, others took service at various time with Egypt's enemies.

The most distinctive piece of Sherden attire was the horned helmet. This bronze helmet did not originally bear the disk located between the horns, but it was worn in Egyptian service, probably as a regimental distinction. The Sherden's armor was of leather studded with metal. Apparently soft leather fastened with leather thongs was used rather than leather which had been hardened by boiling in oil. However, it is possible that the leather armor was either hardened or padded to give greater protection. A short kilt was worn on the lower body with a stiffened, quilted portion in the front, perhaps to offer some protection to the crotch.

The Sherden's primary weapon was the long bronze thrusting or stabbing sword which came to be known as the 'Shardana'. It was actually a descendant of the Bronze Age Levantine dagger. The Sherdens also were sometimes armed with the spear. The round shield was bossed with bronze.

# 2 *Numidian Light Cavalryman*

The Numidians were a nomadic people who lived in what is now Algeria. Virtually growing up on horseback, the Numidians were natural cavalrymen and provided most of Hannibal's light cavalry. At Cannae in 216 BC, for example, the Numidians contributed immensely to Hannibal's greatest victory by driving off a large portion of the Roman cavalry and then helping to 'put the cork in the bottle neck' the Romans found themselves in. When Carthage was finally defeated at Zama in 202 BC, it was primarily because 4000–6000 Numidian cavalrymen (against 4000 or less Numidian cavalrymen who had remained loyal to Hannibal) were hired away from Carthage to fight for Rome by Scipio Africanus. The Romans also used Numidian light infantrymen, who had been trained in North Africa by Roman advisors – a Roman equivalent of a Special Forces A-Team, no doubt ('De Oppresso Liber' is, after all, Latin).

The Numidians, as previously mentioned, were excellent riders who were used primarily as light cavalry skirmishers who would charge, throw their javelins, and then retreat. They were also excellent at ambushes, especially those planned by Hannibal, a master of such tactics. The Numidian was at home on his horse and hence did not need a saddle or bridle, but only a rawhide or rope strap around the neck of the animal as illustrated. Knee pressure and shifting of weight were probably sufficient to cause the horse to change direction as the rider galloped towards the enemy hurling his javelins.

Normal attire for the Numidians was a short, sleeveless, unbleached tunic gathered at the waist by a belt and often affixed at the shoulders by broaches. While riding, the tunic was normally tucked up through the belt. There are indications that Numidian leaders – such as the figure illustrated – wore a leopard-skin head band as a badge of rank.

The Numidian's primary weapon was the javelin, of which

he would carry a reasonable number. Normally, all but the javelin ready to be thrown would be carried behind the shield in the shield hand. The shield was of hide and was unbossed. As a secondary weapon, a dagger or ax was sometimes carried.

---

# 3 Greek Mercenary Hoplite

The hoplite was the most formidable foot soldier of his time. These Greek heavy infantrymen specialized in maneuvers in the closely-packed phalanx. This tightly-packed rectangular formation, up to eight ranks deep with massed spears pointing forward, was very hard for an enemy to stand against. Hoplites served as mercenaries for city states other than their own and for the Persians against other Greeks. During the Macedonian Wars, mercenary hoplites fought for and against Alexander. Frequently, the Greek mercenary hoplites were the only portion of a Persian army which could stand against other Greek heavy infantry. At the Battle of Cunaxa in 401 BC the Persian king Cyrus had 14,000 Greek mercenaries in his employ. Later under Darius III, the Greek mercenary hoplites provided Alexander's only stiff opposition at the battles of Granicus in 334 BC and Issus in 333 BC. At the Battle of Gaugamela in 331 BC Alexander himself had 8–10,000 Greek mercenaries in his employ, while Darius, who had a well-deserved reputation for running and leaving the mercenaries unsupported, was down to only 2000 Greek mercenaries in his employ.

To purchase the hoplite's equipment, known as the 'panoply', was rather expensive; hence, the hoplite was normally a rather well-to-do citizen. Of course, as a well-paid mercenary, the cost could be quickly recovered. The mercenary hoplite, as did all hoplites, had to train extensively so that he could maneuver with the rest of his phalanx.

Since each hoplite purchased his own equipment, there was

quite a diversity. This is especially true of helmets. The figure illustrated wears a type known as 'Chalcidian'. Made of bronze, this helmet, as were most other hoplite helmets, is decorated with a horsehair crest. Various types of armor were also worn, but most common by the fourth century BC – when this figure dates from – was the light cuirass of leather with metal plates for reinforcement or, in the case of the figure illustrated, of layered linen or canvas glued together. These layered cloth cuirasses were also often reinforced with metal plates. The bottom fringe of leather or layered cloth 'pteruges' (feathers) was also sometimes reinforced with metal plates. The greaves were of bronze and were 'sprung' onto the legs rather than being tied or buckled.

The hoplite shield, known as the 'hoplon' or 'aspis', was of wood covered with bronze and was carried as shown, with the arm thrust through a loop and with the hand gripping a handle. The shield, which was intended to protect the hoplite's left and the man to his left's right when in formation, was up to 3 feet in diameter and usually had a polished bronze face with an individual or city blazon painted on. The principal weapon of the hoplite was the long thrusting spear of up to 9 feet in length. The secondary weapon was an iron sword with bronze fittings normally carried on a baldric.

---

# 4  Cretan Archer

Because the Greeks considered the decisive arm in battle the hoplite and Macedonians considered the decisive arm the cavalry, neither emphasized missile troops. The wars against the Persians, however, had proved to them the value of troops who could engage their enemy from a distance. As a result the Greeks, the Macedonians, the Successors (to Alexander), and the Romans all hired archers from the island of Crete, who were considered the best bowmen of their time. Despite their skills and combat value, however, there were rarely large numbers of Cretan archers committed to battle. Alexander had only 500 of them, for example, at Granicus in 334 BC, while at Issus in 333 BC and Gaugamela in 331 BC, he had only 1000 Cretan archers. Perhaps one reason larger numbers were not hired is that Cretan mercenary archers had a reputation for treachery.

This figure wears a soft hat and a short tunic with leather sandals typical of the ancient Mediterranean world. There are indications that, in earlier times at least, Cretan archers wore a distinctive red tunic, though this was by no means universal. Sometimes they also carried a small shield known as a 'pelta' and widely used by light troops in Greek armies.

The bow used by the Cretan archers was a composite bow made of a wood skeleton with strips of horn glued to its belly and then bound with sinew which was also glued to the bow. This process produced a strong bow with a range of up to 200 yards. The arrows used by the Cretans had a broad-headed, barbed, bronze arrowhead and were not considered too effective against armor. The Cretan archers faced a perennial problem of foot archers — lack of sufficient quantities of arrows; however, the Cretans were well-known for picking up the spent arrows of enemy archers and firing them back, thus alleviating such shortages on the battlefield.

---

# 5   *Balearic Slinger*

Most ancient armies included slingers among their light or auxiliary troops. Rhodian slingers were normally hired by the Greeks, while Agrianian slingers formed a significant part of Alexander's army. The most famous of the mercenary slingers, however, were those from the Balearic Islands. Balearic slingers formed up to 5 per cent. of Hannibal's armies and also served in limited numbers with Republican Roman armies.

Balearic slingers began training as boys, who were supposedly not fed until they had hit their food with a projectile from their slings. Greek mercenary slingers often used cast lead missiles (some with messages or insults upon them), but the Balearic slingers relied primarily on stones. Missiles hurled by a skilled slinger could travel over 100 yards, could rarely be seen in flight, and could strike with such force – especially the lead ones – that they imbedded themselves beneath the skin.

The slinger illustrated wears a simple tunic with leather belt and leather shoes. His sling is a leather strap which was wrapped around the wrist as shown when in use. The leather bag worn over his shoulder carries spare missiles. As a close-quarters weapon, a short sword or – in this case – a dagger was carried.

---

# 6 *Levantine Archer*

Like the Greeks, the Romans found that their reliance on heavy infantry – the Legions – left them in perpetual need of mercenary cavalry or missile troops. The Romans actually hired many barbarian mercenary troops who after serving honorably for 25 years gained Roman citizenship. Numidians and Cretans, among others, served as mercenary archers for the Romans, but under the Empire, the most common archers among the auxiliaries were those from the Middle East, especially from Syria. Formed into units of 500 or 1000, these archers were attached to a Legion to give longer range striking power.

The archer illustrated wears a leather helmet reinforced with iron or bronze and having a leather neck flap, though iron or bronze helmets similar to those worn by legionaries were also used by the auxiliaries. His armor consists of a bronze 'jazeraint' (scale) corselet. Over his lower body he wears a bleached wool skirt. His sandals are of leather.

This archer's primary weapon is his compound bow, the

arrows for which are carried in a quiver on the back, though there are indications some Roman auxiliary archers carried their quivers at the waist. To protect his left wrist from the bow string he wears a leather wrist guard, though some experts believe bronze guards were also used. Though it is not visible, he wears a thumb ring – which was typical of Eastern archers – to aid in drawing the bow. His sword, worn on a baldric, is similar to the Roman legionary 'gladius'.

# 7 Ribaud

The Ribauds, who were also known as 'brigands', formed mercenary bands known as 'Routiers' which roamed the continent of Europe during the twelfth to fourteenth centuries. Most of the Ribauds were from the lower classes and included Brabançons, Aragonese, Navarrese, Moors, et. al. Their leader was known as 'Roi des Ribauds' (King of the Ribauds). When employed, the Ribauds often helped with the baggage, though in battle they could function as fierce but undisciplined light infantry. The Ribauds relied heavily upon plunder for their remuneration. When not employed, the Routiers generally turned to pillaging whatever area they found themselves in.

The Ribaud's equipment was frequently a hodgepodge of items he had looted or picked up from the battlefield, and the figure illustrated is no exception. His iron conical helmet, for example, is apparently a bit large for him and shows a few dents. His 'armor' consists of a padded leather surcoat worn over a quilted gambeson. On his feet he wears leather shoes. The bag he carries is for loot and provisions, the latter generally 'foraged'.

This Ribaud's wooden kite shield, reinforced with iron, has obviously seen better days. His primary weapon is a spear, with a short sword worn on the belt as a secondary arm. Among other weapons likely to be used by the Ribauds were maces, axes, mallets, daggers, bills, or even farm implements such as pitch forks.

# 8 Hun

The Huns were a nomadic people from the steppes of Central Asia. Under Attila – the 'Scourge of God' – they were instrumental in the 'fall' of the Western Roman Empire. Later, however, Huns served as 'Ethnikos' (mercenary light cavalry-men) for the Eastern Empire (Byzantium). Mercenary light cavalry such as the Huns or Moors were normally formed into units of 500 men, of which one or more might be attached to Byzantine armies. At Decimum in 533 AD, for example, the great Byzantine general Belisarius had 1000 Huns among his forces. The Huns were excellent horsemen who were complete-ly at home on their hardy steppe ponies and who could eat or sleep mounted and on the move.

The figure illustrated is typical of the Huns who served with the Byzantines in the sixth century. His hair is worn long and his cheeks bear the ritual scars which helped give the Huns their fearsome appearance. Possibly as a result of some successful campaigns in Byzantine service and probably indicators that this figure is a chieftain are the gold earrings, bracelets, and belt he wears. The brightly-colored cap with fur trim is typical Hun headgear. His tunic is of wool or goat hair, though field mouse skins might also be used. Jackets or tunics of goatskin were also common. Fur cloaks and/or fur trim on the tunic, as in this case, were also common because of the cold on the steppes. His leggings are of goatskin.

The Huns were primarily horse archers and thus relied heavily on their bows to defeat an enemy while at a distance. As children the Huns hunted field mice with miniature bows to develop their marksmanship. In Attila's time Hunnic bows had been constructed entirely of layers of horn glued together, but whether this type of bow was retained or a more traditional wood and horn composite bow was used while serving with the Byzantines is not certain. A quiver or quivers and a bowcase for one or more bows were carried behind the rider. After the bow, the Hun's primary arm – though it was also useful in dealing with his livestock – was the lasso or whip, which the Hun could skillfully use to unhorse or drag an enemy. Javelins with bone tips were another weapon widely used by the Huns, though this figure carries an iron-tipped lance, probably supplied by his Byzantine employers or captured in battle from an enemy. The shield, worn slung over his shoulder, is of wicker covered with hide.

---

# 9 *Varangian*

The Varangians were Norsemen who served the Byzantine emperors as mercenaries. The first Norse bodyguard for the Eastern Roman emperor was established around 988, and Varangians continued to serve until the late fourteenth century. Originally, Norsemen from Scandinavia or Russia made up most of the Varangians, but as a result of the Norman Conquest of England in 1066, more Anglo-Saxons joined the Varangians during the latter part of the eleventh century.

The Varangians were very highly paid, especially the 'Varangians of the City' who made up the Imperial bodyguard. Many famous Norse warriors were attracted to Byzantium by the chance to make a fortune by serving with the Varangians, but the most famous was, no doubt, Haraldr Siguraarson (Harald Hardrada), the future King of Norway, who was defeated by Harold of England at Stamford Bridge. In addition to the Varangians who guarded the Emperor, there were frequently Varangians assigned to field armies for use as shock troops. When the Emperor went to war, a contingent of Varangians attended him as guardsmen. Because of their backgrounds as seafarers and their skill at warfare afloat, Varangians were also used at times to suppress pirates.

While on duty in the royal residence, the Varangians may have worn a dress uniform consisting of a red tunic and purple cloak, both with gold decoration. A highly decorated sword and shield may also have been worn for such duties. The traditional weapon of Byzantine Imperial life-guards was the rhomphaia – a two-handed, curved sword. At least some Varangians were also armed with this weapon.

The figure illustrated is armed and equipped more for the field than the palace, however. He wears a conical helmet equipped with a nasal over a mail coif and a long mail coat or hauberk. He also wears iron greaves. The purple cloak may be indicative of service as a royal guard, while the broach and 'Thor's Hammer' amulet are traditional Norse adornments. The drinking horn is also typically Norse.

The Varangians used the two-handed ax as their primary weapon, and this figure is no exception. On his belt he carries a sword as his secondary weapon.

---

# 10 *Genoese Crossbowman*

The crossbow was considered such a formidable weapon in its time that a Papal Interdict of 1139 banned its use among Christians. The ban was shortly ignored, however, and Richard I of England is often credited with stimulating its use by hiring mercenary crossbowmen to accompany him on the Crusades, presumably getting around the Papal ban by assuming it was acceptable to use the crossbow against infidels. Because the crossbow required a great deal of skill it was primarily a weapon for professionals and, thus, usually for mercenaries. Although there were professional crossbowmen from many countries probably the best known were the Genoese, who were such an important part of French armies during the

Middle Ages that hiring them was considered the first step in preparing for a campaign. Many of the excellent Genoese crossbowmen were actually sailors trained to use the crossbow while fighting from Genoese galleys but hiring out as infantrymen to France. At Sluys in 1340, however, they fought from shipboard. Among the other important battles in which Genoese crossbowmen formed an important part of the French army were Courtrai (1302), Morlaix (1342), Crécy (1346), Poitiers (1356), and Agincourt (1415).

The Genoese crossbowman illustrated is behind a pavise, which was a large shield used to protect the crossbowman while reloading his weapon. In the case of a large pavise such as this one which was normally used for siege work, it would have been transported by cart. There were smaller pavises, too, which the crossbowman would carry on his back. These could be removed and propped up when needed, or in a fluid battle situation, the light pavise could be left on the back, the crossbowman turning his back to the enemy while reloading.

His helmet is a bassinet with a mail coif. Over his upper body he wears a mail haubergeon covered by a leather brigandine, which has metal plates rivited inside of it. The heads of the rivets form the patterns visible on the leather. He wears no armor on his lower body, though it was fairly common for crossbowmen to wear knee armor. One consideration for the crossbowman was always that his helmet or armor should not restrict his vision or movements necessary to fire his weapon.

In his mouth, ready for use, this figure has a bolt (or quarrel) for his weapon. The quiver on his belt would normally hold about 18 bolts, carried with the tips upwards. Also on his belt is the spanning-hook used for cocking ('spanning') the crossbow. This process was accomplished by inserting the foot in the stirrup as shown and hooking the bowstring with the hook. Pushing downward with the foot would then prepare the weapon for action. The crossbow shown is probably of composite construction, being made of a combination of wood, tendon, and horn, though by the late fourteenth century steel crossbows were in use. As a close-quarters weapon this figure carries a sword; however, axes and short swords or long daggers were also popular.

# 11 Landsknecht

The Landsknechts were originally raised by the Holy Roman Emperor Maximilian I as Imperial troops; however, they soon were taking service as mercenaries. In fact, the Landsknechts established a reputation as pure mercenaries willing to fight for either or both sides in a conflict and the adage, 'No money, no Landsknechts', was widely echoed during the late fifteenth and early sixteenth centuries when these German soldiers of fortune were widely employed.

The Landsknechts were normally raised in regiments of about 4000 men, though this number could vary considerably. The Landsknechts were based on the Swiss pike formations, which were considered the best of their time. There were, in fact, many clashes between the Swiss pikemen and the Landsknecht pikemen, and these battles were always fiercely fought with no quarter given on either side. The Battle of Novara (1513), the Battle of Marignano (1515), and the Battle of Biccoca (1522), the latter in which the Landsknechts combined with the Spanish arquebusiers to defeat the Swiss thus marking their decline, were three of the more well-known encounters between these two premier mercenary units. Among other important battles of the period in which the Landsknechts participated were Ravenna (1512) and Pavia (1524).

Landsknechts were normally contracted for periods of six months and upwards and were paid according to rank and function. A Doppelsöldner, such as the figure illustrated, for example, would be paid twice what a normal pikeman would receive. This bonus was well deserved, though, for the Doppelsöldner was placed in the front or rear rank and had the job of advancing in front of his formation and using his long two-handed sword to cut a swathe through the opposing pikemen. When facing a cavalry charge, the pikemen would move forward and form a hedgehog. There were also some Landsknechts equipped with arquebuses within the formation as well. Landsknecht regiments were highly organized with their own judicial and quartermaster systems and clearly defined leadership. Although there were many Landsknecht leaders of some note, beyond a doubt the best known was Georg von Fründsberg.

The Landsknechts were well-known for their bright, sometimes gaudy, attire. The right to freedom of dress had been granted to them officially, in fact, at the Imperial Diet of Augsburg in 1503. The slashes and feathered hat, striped doublet, striped breeches, striped and varicolored hose, ornate codpiece, and slashed wide-toed shoes are all indications of such freedom of dress in the figure illustrated.

For all of his finery, however, the Landsknecht was a fighting man and a very good one. As a result, he made sure he was equipped with high-quality arms and armor. Although apparently the only armor worn by this Landsknecht is his breastplate, it should be noted that beneath the large hats Landsknechts occasionally wore metal skullcaps or helmets. His Zweihänder (two-handed sword) was about $5\frac{1}{2}$ feet long and required a strong man to wield it effectively. His shorter thrusting sword – the 'Katzbalger' – was very distinctive of the Landsknechts and, though worn on the hip in this illustration, was often worn in front across the stomach.

# 12  Swiss Pikeman

Throughout the fifteenth century the Swiss pikeman dominated the battlefields of France and Burgundy. Swiss citizen soldiers had won independence for their country and had maintained that independence by their military skills, and because of these skills, in 1424 Florence made the Swiss an offer they could not refuse. As a result 10,000 Swiss took service as mercenaries for the Florentines. For the next 100 years, the Swiss would be the most feared mercenary troops in Europe, France being their primary employer during this period.

The fear the Swiss inspired in their enemies was justified, too. They fought a no-quarter war, rarely taking prisoners. In fact, it was a court-martial offense for a Swiss to stop during battle to take a prisoner or plunder a fallen foe. In the fourteenth century the Swiss had relied primarily on the halberd, but by the 1420s had begun to rely on the pike. Swiss pikemen were normally organized into 3 squares – the vanguard, the center, and the rearguard. Crossbowmen and/or arquebusiers usually made up a portion of the vanguard. The Swiss preferred to decide a battle quickly with an advance, relying on their shocking power to crush an enemy. When forced onto the defensive against cavalry, the Swiss formed a hedgehog with the front rank kneeling and pointing their pikes outward, second rank stooped and bracing their pikes on the ground slanting upward, third rank standing with their pikes at waist level, and fourth rank standing and holding their pikes at head level. Not even a heavily-armored knight could press home a charge against such an array of pikes. Unfortunately, the Swiss were not flexible about improving their weapons or tactics, and at the Battle of Bicocca in 1522 they met defeat, thus dispelling their myth of invincibility.

The figure illustrated wears an Italian-style salett with a mail coif. His armor consists of a breastplate with epaulières, rondelles, and taces. The cross painted on the breastplate and sewn on the hose was relatively standard with Swiss troops. The cross on the hose was worn so that it would be visible even if the upper body were covered. Frequently, the hose colors indicated the wearer's canton. The pike was originally between 12 and 15 feet long but by the end of the fifteenth century was often 18 feet in length. Known as a 'Schweizergegen', the sword worn by this figure was very typical of the Swiss pikemen and was a cross between a dagger and a sword.

# 13 Welsh Mercenary Archer

During the twelfth and thirteenth centuries, Welsh mercenary archers provided large contingents in English armies. Edward I especially made use of Welsh archers. At Falkirk in 1298, for example, the English forces included 10,900 Welsh archers.

The figure illustrated is typical of the mercenary Welsh archers of the late thirteenth century. He wears no armor but only a red linen tunic. The single shoe was worn allegedly so that the bare foot could grip better on uneven ground. The single shoe was definitely a Welsh characteristic of this time period but was normally associated with the northern Welsh who were spearmen rather than with the southern Welsh who were archers. Still, there were no doubt archers who adopted this same trick.

The Welsh bow was originally of elm and was the forerunner of the famed English longbow. Arrows were thrust into the belt as illustrated rather than using a quiver. The same belt supports a sword, though some Welshmen chose instead a long, heavy-bladed dagger.

# 14 Companion Man-at-Arms of the White Company

The White Company was composed primarily of Englishmen — many veterans of Poitiers — and flourished in Italy during the last half of the fourteenth century. At its peak the White Company numbered 2500 men-at-arms and 2000 archers, though by 1387 it had shrunk to 500 men-at-arms and 600 mounted archers as age, battle, and internal differences took their toll of the hard-to-replace manpower. In 1364, Sir John Hawkwood, one of the truly great mercenary captains, was elected captain-general of the White Company. In the English

79

fashion, the men-at-arms normally fought dismounted, interspersing themselves with the longbowmen in the well-proven English manner.

Although most members of the White Company did not wear extensive plate armor; what was worn – helmets, shields, breastplates, etc. – was highly polished, thus giving the company its name. The mounted companion man-at-arms illustrated wears a kettle helmet (also sometimes known as a 'war hat') with a mail coif. Beneath the thickly padded white jupon, he wears a mail haubergeon. His legs and feet are unarmored as is his horse.

His weapons consist of a lance, a sword, and a dagger. The companion archers would have substituted the bow for the lance, but would have retained the sword and dagger, though mauls were also popular secondary weapons with English archers.

# 15   Papal Swiss Guardsman

The Swiss Guards were formed in 1506 to protect the Pope and the Vatican and have continued to serve until today. The figure illustrated wears the uniform of the early sixteenth century, consisting of a blue bonnet, blue doublet with puffy sleeves, and white and red patterned, sleeveless jerkin with a long skirt. White hose complete the uniform. The primary weapon for the Guards was the halberd, but this guardsman wears only his sword, noteworthy for its S-quillon.

# 16   Mercenary Artillerist

Beginning in the fourteenth century cannons were used for sieges and, later, in the field. Originally, 'serpentine' powder mixed in the proportions of 41 per cent. saltpeter, 29.5 per cent. sulfur, and 29.5 per cent. charcoal was used, but it had a tendency to separate into its component parts during transport, thus requiring re-mixture at the gun emplacement and offering the danger of ignition from friction during this re-mixing process. In the early fifteenth century 'corned powder', which was produced as a paste, then dried and crumbled, gave vastly improved performance and also increased power, which blew up many cannons. The cannons or bombards of the later fourteenth and fifteenth centuries were primarily of wrought iron and fired stone shot produced by stone masons and sometimes coated with lead to protect the gun's bore. Depending upon the size of the cannon, shot could weigh up to 200 lbs by the end of the fourteenth century and many times that much by the mid-fifteenth century. Since skill, experience, and knowledge were necessary to service these guns, most artillerists were professionals, often under the supervision of a master gunner who not only could lay and fire the guns but could also repair or manufacture them. Germans, Italians, and Frenchmen predominated among master gunners.

The figure illustrated wears a 'kettle' helmet over a mail coif. His leather 'jack' worn to offer a certain amount of protection against flame, covers a short mail haubergeon. Tucked into his belt are: his only weapon – a dagger, a mallet used for hammering wedges beneath the barrel of his gun to change elevation, and a match or 'touch' on a long handle for igniting the powder charge. He carries a relatively small stone shot, probably for a field gun since siege guns normally used larger shot. His eye patch is probably indicative of an injury suffered from an exploding gun, a common occupational hazard with gunners of the Middle Ages.

---

# 17 *Condottieri*

Although there is not a clear embarkation date between the

Free Companies in Italy and the Condottieri companies (in fact, the terms are often used interchangeably during the second half of the fourteenth century), by the late fourteenth century, the Condottieri had begun to achieve prominence. Condottieri were mercenary captains with their own companies of professional soldiers – primarily cavalrymen, though some infantrymen and occasionally artillerymen were also included in the larger companies. The Condottieri took their name from their contracts of employment – the 'condotta'. A Condottieri could command a small company of only a few 'lances' (The term 'lance' seems to have been brought to Italy by the English companions and normally meant a mounted man-at-arms, though not necessarily a knight, with a squire and a page.), or a large company of several hundred or even more than a thousand men. Such large companies were generally broken into squadrons – often commanded by lesser Condottieri contracted to a greater Condottieri. The largest squadron in the company was usually the 'casa' which included the administrative staff and a hard core of professional fighting men who acted as the personal bodyguard for the Condottieri. The importance of a group of loyal retainers should not be undervalued because of the treacherous atmosphere in Italy during the fifteenth century. More than one well-known Condottieri lost his life by being too trusting. Although the size of the squadrons was not set, by the late fifteenth century 20–25 lances usually comprised a squadron.

All Italian city states needed to employ Condottieri, though Florence, which maintained a rather inefficient and under-strength professional army, had to pay the highest prices because of her greater need. The Condottieri had a reputation for being over-cautious in battle, preferring maneuver and siege to decisive and bloody battle. There is much truth in these criticisms, too, since it was to the Condottieri's advantage to keep an army in the field as long as possible to keep getting paid and to avoid casualties among his hard-to-replace professional soldiers. 'Condotte' often called for bonuses for more dangerous operations, in fact, to counter this tendency towards inertia. Storming a walled city, for example, carried a bonus of one month's wages.

Certain families became well-known for producing Condottieri, among them: Attendolo, Colonna, Malatesta, Orsini, Sanseverino, Sforze, and dal Verme. Powerful noble families had a vested interest in sending at least some of their number into the ranks of the Condottieri since these soldiers of fortune could – and often did – make or break the rulers of great city states through military might. Marriages between Condottieri families to weld alliances were also rather common. Among the more important battles involving the Condottieri were: Castagnaro (1387), Alessandria (1391), Arbedo (1422), Maclodio (1427), San Romano (1432), Caravaggio (1448), and Molinella (1467).

The figure illustrated wears plate armor of the fifteenth century Italian style. Noteworthy are the coudières (elbow guards) and genouillières (knee guards) of plate. The hautepièce which projects horizontally from his pauldron (shoulder guard) protects his neck from a decapitating sword cut. Although his helm is not visible, it would most likely be an armet. Note that his gauntlets are strapped over soft leather gloves and that in his right hand he carries the gilded baton signifying his rank as captain-general of his company. His horse is armored with a combination of plate – especially the chanfron (face plate) and crinet (neck plates) – and cuir-bouilli, which is leather boiled in oil and molded to shape before hardening.

He carries his sword suspended from a belt around the waist; it was fairly common practice in Italy to also have a chain affixing sword, dagger, mace, etc. to the breastplate so that they would not get lost in battle. This figure does not, however, make use of such a device. A dagger, probably a sharp-pointed rondel, would likely be carried on the other side. Suspended from his saddle he carries a mace.

# 18 *Grand Catalan Companion (Almugavar)*

The Grand Catalan Company was originally formed for service in the War of Sicilian Vespers (1282–1302). At the end of that conflict, Roger de Flor and 6500 Grand Catalan Companions under his command were hired by the Byzantines for service against the Turks. Of this number, about 4000 were Almugavars, who are generally conceded to have been the best infantrymen of their time. The Almugavars were mountaineers from Aragon and Navarre and took their name from the Arabic 'Al-Mughuwir', which roughly translates as 'raiders'. Despite their ferocity, the Almugavars were well-disciplined under leaders they respected such as de Flor and could fight as skirmishers or in formation. Their battle cry, 'Aur! Aur! Desperta ferre!' (Aur! Aur! Iron awake!), struck fear into any opponent who had previously faced them (though most of these individuals were not still among the living) or knew their ferocious reputation.

After arriving in Byzantium, the Almugavars lived up to their reputation, the Catalans killing over 50,000 Turks in engagements at Cyzicus, Philadelphia, and the Iron Gate, while suffering only negligible losses. In 1305, the Byzantine Emperor treacherously murdered de Flor and many of his followers, but the remaining members of the Grand Catalan company took bloody revenge, defeating any Byzantine troops sent against them and eventually ravaging Thrace for two years with little opposition. By 1308 they had moved on to the Duchy of Athens, which at first hired them but which they took over in 1311, establishing a Catalan state which lasted until 1379 and which gave future mercenary captains the idea of taking over their own country.

As this figure illustrates, the Almugavars were tough, raw-boned, shaggy-haired men. Although a few Almugavars wore chain mail, most — like this figure — wore only a short fur jacket over a cloth tunic and breeches. Leather leggings with sandals were the normal footwear. A leather hat was the typical headgear. Worn over the shoulder was a leather bag for carrying provisions.

Armament was fairly standard for the Almugavars. A spear and two javelins, the latter capable of penetrating mail or a helmet at close range, were the principal arms. At his waist he carried a short Iberian sword with which he was particularly adept at slitting enemy throats.

---

# 19 Scots Guardsman — France (c.1700)

As a result of the 'Old Alliance', Catholic Scots had a long tradition of serving as household troops for the French kings. By the early fifteenth century, Scottish Archers of the Guard were already acting as bodyguards to the King of France. Scottish Archers of the Guard also distinguished themselves in battle, serving Louis XI against Burgundy. By the eighteenth century, the minimum period of service in the Company of Scots Guards was six years.

The guardsman illustrated, possibly on duty at Versailles, wears a white haqueton embroidered with gold ornamentation, including the symbol of the 'Sun King' and the royal coat of arms. It is noteworthy that as early as the fifteenth century, Scots Guardsmen were already wearing a highly decorated haqueton. Beneath the haqueton is worn a blue tunic with red cuffs edged in white and having three bars of white lace. The coat had red turnbacks and white lace adornments and was worn over a red waistcoat and red breeches as are visible in this illustration. It should be noted that red and blue were the traditional colors of French household troops. A black, felt tricorne hat edged in white lace and black shoes complete his uniform.

This guardsman is armed with a spontoon and a sword, which is worn on a belt at the left side and is not visible in this pose. For non-ceremonial duties a musket and bayonet would have been carried.

## 20  Private, Regiment Lally (c.1760)

The 'Wild Geese' in French service date from the early seventeenth century, though scattered Irish soldiers of fortune had taken service with the French even earlier. The actual origin of the Irish Brigade in France, however, can be traced to 1690. Originally consisting of five regiments – Butler's, Fielding's, Mountcashel's, O'Brien's, and Dillon's, the Brigade was soon consolidated into just three – Mountcashel's, O'Brien's, and Dillon's. The Irishmen soon established a reputation for reckless bravery, especially in the hand-to-hand fighting at which they excelled. During the War of the Spanish Succession (1701–14), the Wild Geese were widely employed as shock troops and are especially remembered for their heroic defense of Cremona. The Irish Brigade was much depleted, however, at the end of this long war, having suffered heavy losses, and it was necessary for more 'geese' to fly south to France – often via an 'underground railway' – to enlist.

By 1715, there were five Irish infantry regiments serving France – Dillon's, Berwick's, O'Brien's, Lee's, and Dorrington's – and one cavalry regiment – Nugent's. During the War of the Austrian Succession (1740–48), Irish infantry regiments seeing action were: Dillon's, Clare's, Berwick's, Roth's, Lally's, and Bulkeley's, with the valiant bayonet charge by the Irish Brigade being a decisive factor in the victory at Fontenoy (1745). Fitzjames's Irish cavalry regiment also saw action during this war. At Culloden (1746) Irish volunteers from France, including some of Fitzjames's cavalrymen, fought for 'Bonnie Prince Charlie'. During the Seven Years War, the Irish cavalry regiment was so decimated that it was disbanded.

Dillon's Regiment along with chasseurs from the Walsh

Regiment were sent in 1779 to fight in aid of the American cause during the American Revolution. Dillon's Regiment was first used to capture the island of Grenada and then joined the American forces in Georgia. During the French Revolution, most of the Irish Regiments remained loyal to the king and, hence, were disbanded, though scattered Irish battalions served Napolcon later on. Some 'Wild Geese' formerly in the service of France also fought for the English against French revolutionaries.

Very specific information about the uniforms of the Irish regiments in 1761 survives. Infantry regiments Bulkeley, Clare, Dillon, Roth, Berwick, and Lally and cavalry regiment Fitzjames all wore red coats. Additional uniform details and distinctions were as follows:

| Regiment | Collar | Cuffs | Skirts | Lapels | Waistcoat | Breeches | Buttons |
|---|---|---|---|---|---|---|---|
| Fitzjames | — | blue | blue | blue | yellow | white | white |
| Bulkcley | red | green | red | — | green | white | white |
| Clare | yellow | yellow | yellow | yellow | red | white | white |
| Dillon | — | black | white | — | red | white | yellow |
| Roth | — | blue | blue | — | blue | blue | yellow |
| Berwick | black | black | white | — | red | white | yellow |
| Lally | green | green | white. | — | green | white | yellow |

The figure illustrated wears a uniform conforming to the information above about the Regiment Lally. In addition, his tricorne hat bears yellow trim and a white cockade. Over his breeches he wears white spatterdashes. The pouch worn suspended from his left shoulder carries ammunition for his musket which is slung over his right shoulder. On his left side in a double frog he carries a short fusilier's sword and a bayonet. The buff leather sling, straps, and belt were standard with French infantry regiments of the time.

---

# 21  *Private, Regiment Irlanda*

'Wild Geese' were already serving Spain by the end of the

sixteenth century in the 'Tercio Irlanda'. Throughout the seventeenth century, Irishmen served in the Spanish army, intermittently formed into a Tercio Irlanda. At the Battle of the Dunes (1658) the Irish regiments serving Spain saw action. Irish soldiers of fortune continued to gravitate to Spain during the eighteenth century, and in 1718 an Irish Brigade containing the Regiments Irlanda, Hibernia, and Ultonia was formed. The Irish Brigade was used during the War of the Austrian Succession (1740–48). The most noteworthy achievement of the Irish Brigade occurred during the defense of Naples in 1744 when members of the brigade made a heroic bayonet charge which helped drive off the Austrian attackers.

Throughout the remainder of the eighteenth century, the Irish Brigade was used much as later 'foreign legions' would be, being sent wherever there was 'dirty work' to be done. Among other places, the Irish Brigade or regiments thereof saw action in Sicily, North Africa, Portugal, and Brazil. The Hibernia and Ultonia Regiments were sent to Mexico on garrison duty in 1768. Whenever relations with the English were not good, it was also only a matter of time until the Irish regiments were used to blockade Gibraltar. During the American Revolution, the Irish Brigade was used to attack British possessions. Later, during the Napoleonic Wars, the Irish regiments fought heroically as part of Wellington's Peninsular army. In 1818 the Irish regiments were formally disbanded, though to this day regiments within the Spanish army trace their lineage to Irish origins.

The figure illustrated wears the sky blue coat adopted by the Irish regiments in 1802 to differentiate them from Spanish line infantry. The yellow collar, cuffs, lapels, and skirts were distinctions for the Regiment Irlanda. The other two regiments wore similar coats with the following differences: Hibernia had sky blue collars and white buttons, and Ultonia had sky blue lapels. Other distinctions were as for Irlanda. The breeches and cross belts were white with a black leather ammunition pouch. Gaiters and cocked hat, the latter with a red cockade, were also black.

# 22 _Swiss Guardsman, France (c.1740)_

The Swiss Guards in France had a tradition dating back to the fifteenth century and were renowned for their loyalty. In 1792 over 600 of them died defending Louis XVI against the mob storming the Tuileries. Had the King not ordered them to cease firing out of misguided 'humanity', it is likely the well-disciplined Swiss would have won the day despite the overwhelming numbers of the opposition. For a short time after the reinstatement of the French monarchy in 1814 a Swiss Guard was re-formed, but it was only a shadow of its former self.

The figure illustrated wears a grenadier-style of mitre hat bearing the royal arms of France. Red and blue were the traditional colors of French royal guards, and his blue coat with red distinctions, red waistcoat, and red breeches conform to this pattern. The cuffs, by the way, are of red plush. Note that the coat is turned back in both front and rear. Such bright colors were not only decorative but also a virtual necessity on the eighteenth century battlefield where smoke often obscured everything to such a degree that a commanding officer could only see the dispositions of brightly-clad troops. White spatterdashes matching the white embellishments on the coat and waistcoat protect the breeches. The blue garters worn with the spatterdashes make an attractive contrast. An interesting note on the dress of the Swiss Guards is that they retained breastplates into the eighteenth century, though they have obviously been dispensed with by the time of this figure.

On the left side, this figure wears a sword and bayonet in a double frog, while on the opposite hip is a cartridge pouch, in French service normally holding 20 prepared cartridges (usually consisting of powder and bullet in a paper envelope) for his Model 1717 flintlock musket.

# 23 *Panduren von der Trenck*

During her various wars, Maria Theresa used over 60 free corps, legions, etc., but none were as notorious as the Panduren-Corps von der Trenck. Formed in 1741 by Col. Franz Trenck, a free-booting soldier of fortune, the Panduren-Corps von der Trenck was known for its propensity towards rape and pillage but also for its successes at commando-style coups de main. Later, under Major Johann Menzel, the Panduren-Corps supposedly became somewhat more respectable and carried out partisan operations.

Under Trenck, the Pandurens wore a 'uniform' combining characteristics of Hungarian, Austrian, Bosnian, and Turkish military dress. There seem to have been, however, four essential similarities of appearance Trenck's irregulars shared. Most noticeable may have been the shaved head and scalp lock worn by the Panduren-Corps under Trenck. This figure's shaved head and scalp lock combined with the saber cut across his left cheek certainly give him an especially bloodthirsty and ruthless look. Three items of attire also seemed to make up the basis of the Panduren's uniform. These were a black shako, red dolman, and red cloak. The figure illustrated does not wear his shako, but the dolman and cloak are apparent. To round out his uniform, he wears a sash, baggy Turkish-style trousers, and yellow hussar boots.

His armament is also very Eastern in style. In an Ottoman-pattern chest holster he carries a brace of pistols, the powder flask for which is also Turkish in pattern. Tucked into his sash is a kindjal. His saber is also distinctly eastern resembling a Turkish kilij more than a Western cavalry saber.

# 24 Dragoon, Schwarze Brigade Favrat

During the Seven Years War (1756–63), Frederick the Great hired a number of free battalions, especially of light infantry. The records of most of these units were remarkably undistinguished, however, and they were soon disbanded. Of more interest than most was the Schwarze Brigade Favrat (formed 1761) because it contained grenadiers, dragoons, jaegers, and hussars within its ranks.

The figure illustrated wears a black coat with red distinctions. The tricorne hat is also black with a yellow cockade. The waistcoat and breeches are straw-colored. Black leather jackboots complete the uniform.

Within the Schwarze Brigade Favrat uniforms varied depending upon the types of troops. Grenadiers wore the black coat with red distinctions, straw waistcoat, and straw breeches. Jaegers wore a black coat with green distinctions, green waistcoat, and green breeches. Hussars wore a yellow dolman and black pelissc.

This dragoon is loading one of the brace of pistols carried on his saddle. Normally, 18 carbine cartridges and 12 pistol cartridges would have been carried in a pouch at the right hip affixed to the white bandolier passing across his shoulder. His dragoon's carbine – longer than the cavalry carbine but shorter than the infantry musket – would have been slung from this same bandolier when in action. His short dragoon's sword has the distinctive eagle's head pommel unique to the dragoons.

# 25 King's German Legionnaire

The King's German Legion was originally formed in 1803 when former members of the Hanoverian army fled to England after the occupation of their country by the French. The KGL, however, soon became a 'Legion' of true soldiers of fortune by admitting Germans other than Hanoverians, Poles, Hungarians, Danes, and Russians. Eventually, the KGL would consist of eight battalions of line infantry, two battalions of light infantry (Jaegers), three regiments of hussars, two regiments of dragoons, two troops of horse artillery, and four batteries of field artillery. Enlisted members of the KGL served on basically the same terms as British troops. Officers' enlistments were slightly different, however. KGL officers' enlistments stipulated service only in Europe, and promotions could not be purchased in the KGL.

The King's German Legion was originally used primarily for garrison duties but under Wellington in the Peninsula and at Waterloo established a reputation as being equals to any British troops. In fact, the 1st Hussars of the KGL were considered Wellington's best cavalry in the Peninsula, and the two light battalions were rated among the best infantry units.

Uniforms of the KGL were similar to those of equivalent British units. This Jaeger of the 1st Light Battalion, for example, wears a uniform very similar to that of members of the Rifle Corps. A 'rifle green' jacket with black collar, cuffs, and shoulder straps and with a single row of white metal buttons was regulation for the 1st Light Battalion, while the 2nd Light Battalion had three rows of buttons and minor differences in the shoulder straps. The black shako bears a short black plume and a white metal Jaeger horn. Leather equipment is also of black.

The blue water bottle was a well-known Hanoverian item of equipment which was carried over to the KGL. On his left hip this Jaeger also carries a sword bayonet used with the Baker rifle. The pouch over the right hip contains balls and patches to be used when the rifle was carefully loaded for precision shooting. The powder horn on the right hip would also be used for such careful loading. A number of prepared paper cartridges would be carried as well, however, should rapid fire be needed when facing a cavalry charge or in some other situation.

The Baker rifle carried by this figure was in its time considered a very accurate weapon since it was capable of $3\frac{1}{2}$ foot groups at 100 yards. It was a Germanic-style rifle, which made it especially useful for the Jaegers of the KGL. It was a .625 caliber and had a .30 inch barrel. Weight was a little over 9 lbs.

---

# 26 Ninja

In feudal Japan, the Ninja were for hire by the highest bidder to carry out spy missions, sabotage, assassinations, or other acts of espionage and terrorism. These experts at Ninjutsu were skilled with all sorts of weapons and at techniques of infiltration and escape. They were experts at hand-to-hand combat; scaling and climbing; underwater swimming; escape from locked rooms, chains, etc.; remaining immobile for extended periods; impersonations; sleight of hand; hypnosis; and many other skills applicable to their missions. The secrets of the Ninja were normally passed from father to son and, thus, one had to be born into a Ninja clan or adopted into one to become a Ninja.

The figure illustrated wears the black clothing and hood traditionally associated with the Ninja. Since most Ninja infiltrations took place at night, the dark clothing granted better camouflage. Diced stockings and rope sandals complete his attire.

The Ninja made use of many special weapons including collapsible bows, telescoping spears, blowguns, and 'chemical' weapons such as poisoned darts or smoke bombs. The Ninja illustrated has three weapons visible, though it is likely that there are others concealed about his person. Over his back he carries a Daito (long sword), though a shorter sword with a square tsuba (guard) is often associated with the Ninja. The Ninja often used a special sheath for his sword which had a hole at the bottom so he could use the sheath as a breathing tube when hiding under the water of a castle moat or elsewhere submerged. With his right hand he is preparing to throw a 'shaken', or throwing star. These were usually carried in multiples and were used to eliminate sentries or other enemies at a distance or to distract an enemy while launching an attack or retreating. (Note: At least a few special operations units today receive training in the use of a sophisticated version of this weapon.) In his left hand is a kusari-gama, which was a combination of a sickle and chain. In the hands of a skilled user – as the Ninja were – this was a truly formidable weapon, and many Ninja favored it above other weapons. Around his waist he wears a rope to be used for scaling or climbing, though he could also use it as an entangling weapon should the situation demand it.

## 27 Swiss Guardsman, Austria (c.1745)

Although not as large in numbers as the Swiss Guards employed by the French monarchs, there was a unit of Swiss Guards which served Maria Theresa. Their specific duties included mounting interior guards within the royal palaces at the Hofburg and at Schönbrunn.

For normal duties the Swiss Guards wore the uniform illustrated, but for ceremonial occasions a steel helmet, ornamented cuirass, and ornamented halberd were used. The standard hat was the black, felt tricorne with gold lace edging and a black and gold cockade. The ruff, puffed sleeves, and puffed breeches (or 'upper hose') were of renaissance fashion. The basic color for the tunic and breeches was red with black and yellow/gold stripes, thus incorporating the Hapsburg-Lorraine colors of Maria Theresa and her husband. Red hose were worn for everyday duties, while white ones were used with the ceremonial uniform. The black leather shoes have gold and black rosettes. Completing the uniform were tan leather gloves with gold embroidery along the edges.

The standard halberd, as illustrated, was unadorned steel. The sword, suspended from a white leather sword belt, had brass fittings and a brass hilt.

## 28 Major General Friedrich von Steuben

Of the many foreign soldiers of fortune who served the American cause, von Steuben made one of the greatest contributions by serving as the drill master for the Continental Army. Von Steuben had served as an officer in the Prussian Army during the Seven Years War and had been attached to Frederick the Great's general staff. He was recruited by Benjamin Franklin and Silas Deane to help instill Prussian discipline into the new American Army.

He became Inspector General of the Continental Army and helped turn the American farmers and tradesmen into soldiers. He also wrote the tactical manual – 'Regulations for the Order and Discipline of the Troops of the United States' – which became the training guide for the Continental Army.

As per the orders of June, 1780, von Steuben wears the blue coat with buff facings, buff waistcoat, and buff breeches. The epaulettes bear the two stars of a major general. The black and white feather in the hat was also distinctive of major generals. Among the orders he wears is the Prussian Order of the Black Eagle around his neck.

## 29 Hesse-Cassel Jaeger

The Jaegers were probably the most effective of all German mercenary troops used in the American Revolution since they were skilled woodsmen able to compete on an equal footing with American woodsmen. 17,000 Hessians served in North America during the Revolution, most very high quality troops equal to those of Prussia, which were usually considered the best of their time. Of this number, however, no more than 5–600 were Jaegers. The Jaegers were recruited from among gamekeepers, foresters, and huntsmen and were skilled trackers and marksmen. They served as scouts, skirmishers, point or rear guards, and snipers. Because of their versatility and usefulness, small groups of Jaegers were normally attached to Hessian units going into battle, and thus Jaegers could count among their battle honors: Flatbush, White Plains, Trenton, Brandywine, and Yorktown. Despite the American propaganda about German mercenaries, the Hessians actually were well-disciplined and rarely had problems with the local population. In fact, thousands of Hessians settled in America at the end of the war, hardly possible for a group of 'war criminals'.

There were both mounted and foot Jaegers. The figure illustrated is from one of the foot Jaeger companies. Green was the traditional color of Jaeger units having first been adopted by the Prussian Field Jaeger Corps in 1744. It was also the traditional color of German huntsmen and thus especially appropriate. The green coat with red facings, green waistcoat, and green breeches were the standard uniform for the Jaegers from Hesse-Cassel. In hotter weather buff or white breeches were normally substituted for the green ones, and mounted Jaegers wore leather breeches. The tricorne hat beats a green cockade.

Leather equipment was buff. Instead of a bayonet the Jaegers carried a traditional hunting cutlass, normally as illustrated with a hunting knife carried in a second sheath affixed to the front of the cutlass scabbard. In hand-to-hand fighting, this lack of a bayonet occasionally put the Jaegers at a disadvantage, but they were not meant to fight as line infantry. The Jaegerbusche rifle was shorter than American long rifles and thus did not have their range, but it was quite accurate in the hands of the Jaegers, who were normally expert marksmen.

Generally, the rifle was the Jaeger's personally-owned weapon, and he was quite familiar with it as a result.

# 30 Hussar Lauzun's Legion

The Lauzun's Legion was originally formed in 1778 and took part in the capture of Senegal in December, 1778. Composed primarily of Germans, Poles, and Irishmen, the Lauzun's Legion was definitely a 'foreign legion', orders even being given in German rather than French. Nine hundred men of the Lauzun's Legion, including grenadiers, chasseurs, fusiliers, gunners, and hussars, were sent to North America in 1780 as part of the French expeditionary forces under Rochambeau. The Lauzun's Legion hussars formed a large part of the French cavalry sent to North America and were used to scout and carry out reconnaissance for the French Army.

The figure illustrated wears the blue dolman with yellow lace and braid and blue pelisse distinctive of the Lauzun's Legion hussars. His Hungarian-style hussar's breeches are yellow, though at various times during their existence, the Lauzun hussars also seem to have worn red and blue breeches. His black shako is decorated with gold braid. Black hussar's boots complete the uniform.

His equipment includes a saber, sabretache, and cartridge pouch. Attached to the red sash or belt across his chest is the Model 1777 Cavalry 'Mousqueton'.

# 31 General de Brigada Lee Christmas

Lee Christmas first went to Honduras in 1894 as a railway engineer, but when his train was captured by revolutionaries led by General Duron, Christmas was drafted at gunpoint into the rebel army. Though recruited under duress, Christmas soon proved to be a valuable addition to Duron's army as he constructed an armored train car and later a fortress of ice blocks for the rebels. Though it seems ridiculous in the tropical heat, Christmas's ice fortress helped the rebels defeat a force of federal troops which had been sent to crush them. Christmas, who was now a trusted officer of the revolutionary army, fled to Nicaragua when Duron's army was defeated a short time later.

Before long, however, Christmas was invited back to Honduras to head the federal police. In January, 1903, he brought the police force into the fold of Manuel Bonilla who had been elected president but who was facing another civil war against the forces of the previous regime. Christmas was given the command of Bonilla's army, which he led to victory.

Now a general, Christmas defeated two other rebel armies, but when Bonilla's forces were defeated, Christmas was captured by an invasion force from Nicaragua. He soon managed to escape to Guatemala, however, where he re-established contact with Bonilla and began planning for a return to Honduras. In 1911 he led Bonilla's re-formed army on an amphibious operation which allowed them to re-take control of the country. Christmas remained in Honduras until 1917 when a change in regimes meant that he was no longer welcome.

Christmas is depicted in the highly ornate uniform he was presented after leading Bonilla's forces to victory the first time. The abundant braid and brocade are typical of Latin American uniforms of the period as are the highly-polished, black boots. The képi is also heavily braided. In the field, Christmas wore a more utilitarian gray corduroy uniform.

# 32 *Major, Madras Engineers (c.1840)*

For about a century before 1858, British officers hired themselves out to the East India Company to command Indian troops employed by the Company for the defense of the sub-continent.

For many reasons service in the forces of the East India Company held great appeal for the soldier of fortune. Very importantly for officers with middle class backgrounds, service in the Indian Army did not require an independent income just to keep up social obligations and appearances. Many British regiments, on the other hand, required that an officer spend far more than he earned on uniforms, horses, mess fees, etc. Promotion within the Indian Army also came faster and was based much more on merit than were promotions in the British Army where promotions could be purchased rather than won on the battlefield. Perhaps most appealing of all, though, to the true soldier of fortune was the chance to serve in an exotic land where there were fortunes to be made and where there was a chance to see a great deal of combat.

Though there was far more romance attached to serving with one of the colorful Indian cavalry regiments such as Skinner's Horse, British officers also served in the more technical arms of the East India Company's forces such as the Engineers, Artillery, and Medical. The armies of each of the three presidencies – Bengal, Madras, and Bombay – had their own separate support arms.

The officer illustrated, from the engineers of the Madras Army, wears the dress uniform stipulated in the 1838 Dress Regulations. The cocked hat bears a white swan's feather over a foot long. The scarlet, double-breasted coatee has buttons which taper from 3 inches apart at the top to $2\frac{1}{2}$ inches apart at the bottom of the coat. The cuff and collar patches are of blue velvet and are both ornamented with braid. Epaulettes are of gold. The trousers are dark blue with gold stripes. A crimson, silk sash is worn around the waist. Over this sash is a leather belt with gold embroidered stripes. The sword is of the infantry pattern.

---

# 33 *Philhellene*

Roughly translated 'philhellene' means lover of Greece and is the term normally applied to those soldiers of fortune who flocked, between 1821 and 1827, to aid Greece in her fight for independence from Turkey. One of the most famous of the Philhellenes was Lord Byron, but there were others whose actual military contributions were greater. Admiral Lord Cochrane, who had already served as a sailor of fortune in the Chilean and Brazilian navies, for example, commanded the Greek fleet. Although many of the Philhellenes were very altruistic, it should be noted that Cochrane demanded payment of £37,000 before taking command and an additional £20,000 to be put in trust and paid when the Greeks had won their independence. Another well-known British Philhellene was Sir Richard Church, who took over command of the Greek ground forces in the last years of the war.

Probably the most famous of the French Philhellenes was Charles Fabvier, a former officer under Napoleon who headed a small 'free company' composed primarily of Italian and French exiles. Between 1824 and 1825, Fabvier led these exiles to Greece. Since many of them were former professional soldiers, they formed the basis for a Greek regular army under Fabvier's command. By the end of 1825, Fabvier could field 3500 trained regular troops, but he was later superseded by Church as the commander of the Greek 'regulars'.

The list of Philhellenes could go on, but the men already discussed were typical of the breed. Almost 1000 Philhellenes fought for Greece during the Greek War of Independence, almost one-third dying in Greece. The largest number of Philhellenes were Germans, of which 342 fought for Greece. Many of this number had joined the 'German Legion' formed in 1822 but which had drifted into oblivion by 1823 through various 'snafus'. Other nationalities represented in some numbers included: French – 196, Italians – 137, British – 99, Swiss – 35, Poles – 30, Dutch and Belgians – 17, and Americans – 16.

Many of the Philhellenes designed their own uniforms and had them tailored to their specifications. Lord Byron, for example, had an entire wardrobe of gaudy uniforms tailored and wore a helmet patterned on those of classical Greece. As a result many uniforms represented the romantic idea that some Philhellenes had about war rather than any reality. The Greek War of Independence took place shortly after the Napoleonic Wars, which had been a period of highly ornate military dress as well. Many officers were veterans of these wars and thus wore uniforms reminiscent of those they had worn in their days of glory. The figure illustrated dates from the earlier period of the Greek War of Independence (c.1822) and wears a uniform typical of the Philhellenes of this period. Obvious Napoleonic influences are apparent in the shako, coatee, breeches, and boots. German, French, and British influences are all apparent in the uniform's styling. The officer's gorget – a rank distinction on its way out by this period – is visible around the figure's neck.

## 34 Rifleman, 2nd Gurkha Rifles (late nineteenth century)

The 2nd Gurkha Rifles – the 'Prince of Wales' Own' (later 'King Edward VII's Own') – is the senior Gurkha regiment within the British Army having been founded in 1815. During the late nineteenth century, from whence the figure illustrated dates, the 2nd Gurkha Rifles were heavily involved in warfare along the North West Frontier, serving, among other assignments, as part of the Kandahar Field Force.

The figure illustrated wears the traditional Gurkha pillbox hat with the red and white dice band of the 2nd Gurkhas. The regimental cap badge bears the Prince of Wales' plume. The tunic and trousers are both rifle green, with the tunic having red braid on the collar and red piping on the cuffs. A black leather belt with a 'snake' fastening carries the bayonet on the left hip and the kukri on the right hip.

His weapon is the Martini-Henry rifle, which during the period of this rifleman was being replaced by the Lee-Metford. The piece of leather in the left hand may well be for use in holding the rifle's fore-end since the Martini-Henry had a reputation for overheating in rapid fire. The Gurkhas, it should be noted, have long held a reputation as excellent riflemen, often winning Army-wide rifle matches.

# 35 *Gurkha Rifleman, World War I*

By 1914, one-sixth of the Indian Army was composed of Gurkhas – a tribute to their fighting ability – and all ten Gurkha regiments saw action during World War I, some battalions serving in France and some in the Middle East. In France 'Neuve Chapelle' especially stands out as a battle in which the Gurkhas distinguished themselves. Among the many battle honors added by the Gurkhas in the Middle East was Gallipoli, where a detachment of Gurkhas was the last unit to pull out.

The figure illustrated wears the khaki jacket, shorts, and puttees issued for hot weather wear in India. Those battalions serving in France, however, were soon issued warmer woolen clothing. The slouch hat had come into use with the Gurkha regiments early in the twentieth century and was widely worn during World War I. This figure wears the 1903 Bandolier Equipment, which though replaced in general issue by the

102

1908 pattern equipment was still issued in India and the Middle East and was likely to be encountered in use by the Gurkha regiments during at least the early years of the war. The haversack of this equipment is visible on the left hip supported by a webbed strap passing over the right shoulder. The bandolier had five pockets, each of which held two, five-round stripper clips of .303 ammunition. The waist belt held an additional four pockets, two of which each held two stripper clips and two of which each held three stripper clips. In all, 100 rounds could thus be carried in this equipment. The kukri was carried on the right side of this belt.

In his left hand this figure carries his Lee-Enfield rifle, while in his right hand he carries the kukri ready for use. It should be noted, by the way, that Gurkhas serving in France soon made the Germans believers in the effectiveness of the kukri in the close-quarters fighting in the trenches and in 'no-man's-land'. Reportedly, more than one English officer with the Gurkhas also got his chance to see if it was possible to decapitate an enemy with one blow of the kukri; it was!

# 36 Subadar-Major, 3rd Gurkha Rifles (c.1905)

The 3rd Gurkha Rifles are now part of the new Indian Army but at the time of the figure illustrated were part of the Imperial Indian Army. At that time Subadar-Major was the highest rank a VCO (Viceroy Commissioned Officer) could achieve. 'Native' officers – the VCOs – were paid less than British officers and remained subordinate to them. After 1917, however, Indian officers graduating from Sandhurst became KCIP (King's Commissioned Indian Officers) and those graduating from the Indian Military Academy at Dehra Dun became ICO (Indian Commissioned Officers) and were of equal status with British officers.

The officer illustrated wears rifle green pillbox hat, tunic, and trousers. The tunic bears black braid at the collar and cuffs.

He wears the pouch belt of the 3rd Gurkha Rifles and black 'seal leather' waist belt with buckle bearing crossed kukris. His sword is the British 1895 pattern. The two medals being worn are the Indian Order of Merit and the India Medal.

# 37 Legionnaire, RMLE, World War I

Almost 43,000 Legionnaires served on the Western Front during World War I, of which more than 30,000 became casualties. Early in the war the Legionnaires served in various régiments de marche, but late in 1915 the Legion units fighting in France were formed into the RMLE (Régiment de Marche de la Légion Étrangère). Although some German, Austrian, Bulgarian, and Turkish Legionnaires volunteered to fight against their own countries, most from the Central Powers served in North Africa during the war. Some Legionnaires also served in the Dardanelles.

The figure illustrated wears the khaki uniform which had become relatively standardized for Legionnaires on the Western Front by early 1916. The Adrian steel helmet with infantry grenade as insignia had replaced the képi for combat. The basic uniform consisted of a single-breasted tunic, breeches, puttees, and a greatcoat. The greatcoat was normally worn as illustrated with the skirts buttoned back. Regimental numbers would normally be worn on the collar tops of the greatcoat though they are not visible here. The green chevrons on the left upper sleeve each represent 6 months service in the war zone.

Over his shoulder this Legionnaire wears the musette bag and a rolled tent. Over his hipbones are leather cartridge pouches. His rifle is the 8 mm M1886/93 'Lebel'.

# 38 *French Foreign Legion Caporal, Solferino (1859)*

During the Second War of Italian Independence, the 2nd RE fought in two important battles against the Austrians – Magenta on 4 June 1859, and Solferino on 24 June 1859. In both cases the Legionnaires showed the courage and tenacity for which they would become famous.

The figure illustrated wears the képi pattern which had been introduced in 1858 with a brass '2', the regimental number. His blue greatcoat has dark blue écussons on the collar and two crimson stripes denoting rank on the sleeve. Epaulettes were also worn on the greatcoat as shown. His medals are worn pinned to the left breast of the greatcoat and include the Médaille Militaire and the Crimean Medal. Beneath the greatcoat would be worn a blue tunic with a crimson collar piped in blue. This figure wears the crimson trousers worn in cold weather; white ones were worn in hot weather. White gaiters complete the uniform.

Visible equipment includes the water bottle and leather belly pouch associated with the Legion in the Crimea and Italy. Sticking up from the knapsack are the two halves of his tent pole. Not visible would be the 1831 short saber, which as a corporal he would probably carry along with his bayonet on the left hip. The Legion has traditionally been more than willing to close with the enemy and use the bayonet, and this corporal is no exception, having the bayonet fixed on his 1853 pattern percussion musket.

# 39 *Caporal-chef, 3rd REI, Morocco (1930s)*

In 1920 the RMLE was redesignated the 3rd REI (Régiment Étrangère d'Infânterie). Throughout the 1920s and early 1930s, the 3rd REI was involved in establishing and garrisoning

French outposts in Morocco. Battalions of the 3rd REI were also involved in the Riff War during the 20s.

The figure illustrated wears the famous white képi cover – the 'képi blanc' – over his képi. The khaki tunic and trousers are retained along with the khaki greatcoat and puttees worn during World War I. Note that regimental numbers are worn on the collar tips of the greatcoat and rank insignia is worn on the cuffs; all insignia are in green. On the left shoulder he wears the unit fourragère of the Croix de Guerre. He also wears his own medals, including the Croix de Guerre-TOE, on his left breast.

His weapon is the Model 1924/29 'Chatellerault' machine-gun. This 7.5 mm. weapon was actually a reasonably good choice for the Legion since at just over 20 lbs it could be carried relatively easily by an infantryman. The box magazine at the top of the weapon held 25 rounds. As a secondary weapon he carries the Model 1892 revolver in a hip holster.

# 40 *T.E. Lawrence*

Thomas Edward Lawrence – 'Lawrence of Arabia' – studied archaelogy at Oxford and spent several years before World War I digging and traveling in the Middle East. When World War I began he received a commission in the British army and served in the Middle East as a staff officer. In 1916, however, he found his true calling as a 'soldier of fortune' when he was sent to help foment an Arab revolt against the Turks. He soon gained the respect of Abdulla, the Sherif of Mecca, and his brother Hussein. With Hussein, Lawrence then led the Bedouins in a highly successful guerilla campaign against the Turks. After the war ended, Lawrence, by then a colonel, left the Army and wrote. In 1922 he joined the RAF, in which he spent most of the remaining years until his death in 1935.

Though Lawrence wore Arab dress, he did not attempt to

disguise himself as an Arab. Surprisingly, he did not convert to Islam either yet was followed despite being a Christian. Lawrence did believe that it was important to dress as befitting a sherif so that he looked like a leader and, hence, chose high-quality clothing.

In this illustration, for example, he wears a white silk 'kuffieh' over his head with a gold and silver wire 'agal' to hold it in position. Though his flowing white robes could be termed an 'aba', strictly speaking these were under robes, over which he often wore a black camel's hair 'aba'. On the gold brocaded belt at his waist he wears a silver jambiya which is filigreed with gold inlay. Although Lawrence is barefoot in this illustration he always made it a point to wear boots in the 'snake belt' of the North African Desert.

A final comment on Lawrence's attire should be made about the clothing he reportedly wore when carrying out reconnaissance missions behind Turkish lines. On such operations, he supposedly dressed as an outcast Arab woman when passing Turkish checkpoints. His small stature no doubt stood him in good stead in such situations. Once through the lines when actually walking around in Turkish occupied cities, he supposedly wore his British officer's uniform with the insignia removed, relying on the Turks to assume he was a German.

# 41  *Lt Gen. John Glubb*

The Arab Legion was the direct descendant of Lawrence's Arab Army and had been guided during its early years by another British soldier of fortune, F.G. Peake. John Glubb had served as an officer in the Royal Engineers in France during World War I, being wounded three times, once in the jaw which left a life-long mark. After the war, he served in Iraq where he became an expert on tribal law. He also studied Bedouin customs and Arabic and even traveled across the desert by camel. Because of the constant tribal warfare in Transjordan, Glubb was invited to come there in 1930 to help solve the problem. By 1931 Glubb's famous Desert Patrol formed of Bedouins was in operation, and by 1932 the raiding had ceased, to a large extent as a result of the force of Glubb's personality.

In 1939 upon Peake's retirement Glubb took over command of the Arab Legion. He commanded it during World War II and the 1948 Arab–Israeli War and building upon Peake's foundation established the Arab Legion as the best Arab army in the Middle East. Due to internal Jordanian politics, at least partially resulting from the influx of Palestinians, Glubb was forced to retire by King Hussein in 1956 and shortly thereafter the other British officers serving with the Arab Legion left as well. Many believe that if Glubb had been so inclined he could have taken over the country, but his loyalty to the king, as was the Arab Legion's, was beyond doubt.

Glubb wears the standard Arab Legion 'shemagh' with black 'agal' and the Arab Legion cap badge. His tunic, shirt, tie, and trousers make up the khaki drill summer-weight service dress. With it he wears a Sam Browne belt. Though not visible, on his shoulder straps he wears the rank insignia of a lieutenant general. His ribbons include both British and Transjordanian awards.

# 42 *Tracy Richardson*

Tracy Richardson was one of America's most adventurous soldiers of fortune and was in demand throughout Latin America during the early twentieth century for his skills with the machine-gun. Richardson, who fought for at least seven different countries during his life, first took service with Nicaraguan revolutionaries in 1909. Among his adventures during that revolution were the single-handed 'capture' of Managua through a bluff and the elimination as a fighting force of an entire Nicaraguan government regiment by Richardson and another machine-gunner.

In 1911 he joined Venezuelan revolutionaries but was recruited away by another famous soldier of fortune, Gen. Lee Christmas, to fight for the Honduran Bonillaists as a colonel under Christmas. From Honduras he moved on to serve in Mexico under Salazar and Campa. He joined American troops landing at Vera Cruz in 1914, serving General Funsten as an 'intelligence officer'. After that he spent a short time in Guatemala.

Shortly after the outbreak of World War I, Richardson went to Canada and joined the Princess Patricia's Canadian Light Infantry as a machine-gunner, and by 1915 was in action in France where he was wounded. After recuperating he received a commission and transferred to the British Royal Naval Air Service and he served as a pilot. After the USA entered the war, Richardson transferred once again in 1918 and became a pilot in the US Air Service. Between the wars he held various jobs ranging from mine manager to prohibition agent, but in 1941 he rejoined the US Army Air Corps and served until 1946 when he was discharged as a LTC. Richardson died a few years later.

Richardson is illustrated during the period 1909–12 as a free-lance machine-gunner in Latin America. His hat, neckerchief, blue workshirt, and trousers are a uniform only in the sense that they were fairly standard attire for adventurers along the Tex-Mex border at that time. His handgun is a Colt Single Action Army revolver, probably in .45 Colt caliber. Richardson's foot rests upon one of the weapons which helped make him famous as the 'World's Greatest Machine-Gunner', in this case, the Hotchkiss.

---

# 43 Major General Frank 'One-Arm' Sutton

Frank Sutton served as an officer in the Royal Engineers during

World War I, losing an arm to a grenade he was attempting to throw back at Gallipoli while in action alongside a group of Gurkhas. Despite having his hand blown off, Sutton managed to dispatch a Turk who had come to finish him off by biting the Turk's ear off as he grabbed a kukri with his left hand and plunged it into the Turk's throat. After finishing the war working on inventions in Britain and the US, Sutton dredged for gold in Siberia during 1919, and in 1921 went to China. Shortly after arriving there, he began attempting to sell his modification of the Stokes Gun (a type of trench mortar). He was hired by Gen. Yang Sen to manage his private arsenal. After leaving Yang Sen's employ Sutton was hired in 1922 by the 'Old Marshal' Chang Tso-lin to run the Mukden Arsenal. Sutton gained the old warlord's confidence and was entrusted with the direction of intelligence operations and with carrying out some sensitive espionage missions personally. He was also given command of some of the Marshal's forces in the field, including those which breached the Great Wall under Sutton's personal direction. As a result of Sutton's successes in the field he was promoted to major general. He left the 'Old Marshal's' service in 1927.

Sutton's adventurous career was not over, however. He continued his interest in armaments design, and in 1932 he fabricated an armored vehicle based on a surplus artillery tractor chassis and named it the 'Sutton Skunk'. Expecting this vehicle to sell well in China, Sutton returned to market it but was unsuccessful. To earn a living he then became a war correspondent for the Hearst papers covering fighting between Japan and China following the Mukden Incident. Sutton remained in the Far East for the next few years – primarily in Korea where he ran afoul of the Kempei Tai (the Japanese secret service) – and was taken prisoner by the Japanese when Hong Kong fell. He died in 1944 in a Japanese concentration camp.

Sutton is illustrated in the service of the 'Old Marshal'. His tunic, which bears Chinese major general's rank insignia, breeches, and leather leggings are of British style. He retains the Sam Browne belt and often wore his Military Cross. Sutton normally was armed with one or more revolvers – multiples being carried in combat because of the difficulty he had reloading – but is illustrated loading the Model 1896 Mauser he purchased after an attempt on his life in 1925. When driving Sutton normally mounted the Mauser on the left side of his vehicle where he could spray any ambushers with it.

## 44 Major, Bolivian Army (Chaco War)

Between 1932 and 1935 Paraguay and Bolivia fought one of the least known conflicts of the twentieth century – the Chaco War. This war, which involved over 400,000 men and was fought over a jungle known as the 'Gran Chaco' which lay on the borders of both belligerents, cost over 100,000 lives. Although Bolivia had a far larger, better-trained, and better-equipped army than the Paraguayans; the Bolivians, being mostly highlanders, were not as well acclimatized to the jungles as the Paraguayans and could not defeat the lesser power. After a successful counter-offensive by the Paraguayans, the war turned into a stalemate, which was finally settled by a peace agreement in 1938 awarding Paraguay most of the disputed territory.

Both sides in the Chaco War employed foreign soldiers of fortune as officers. Germans, Czechs, Spaniards, and Chileans served the Bolivians, while French, British, and White Russians served the Paraguayans.

The figure illustrated is one of the ubiquitous Germans serving Bolivia. The gray-green peaked cap bears the Bolivian officers cap badge. On the collar tips of the gray-green tunic he wears scarlet tabs indicating service on the general staff; the collar insignia also denotes general staff. Other branch colors included: red – infantry, black – artillery, green – cavalry, red violet – engineer, dark blue – air corps, light brown – quartermaster, pale violet/gray – medical. Major's rank insignia worn on the shoulder also includes the scarlet stripe indicating general staff service. The gray-green riding breeches are tucked into riding boots worn with spurs. On the belt he wears a Walther PP 7.65 mm. automatic pistol.

# 45 *Frank Tinker (Spanish Civil War)*

Frank Tinker, a former US Navy pilot, was one of 17 Americans who flew for the Republicans in Spain. Flying the Soviet I.15 'Chato' and the I.16 'Mosca', Tinker was one of two Americans to become an ace for the Republicans. Tinker's score eventually reached eight, including two Me-109s. The other American ace, Albert J. Baumler, later served with the Flying Tigers and became an ace with the USAAF in World War II as well. By the fall of 1937, enough Spanish pilots had been trained in Russia so that Tinker did not renew his contract (which, by the way, had carried a $1000 bonus for each enemy plane shot down) and returned to the USA.

Tinker's flying gear consists of flying helmet and goggles and a heavy leather flying suit. Since the aircraft flown by Tinker and other members of the 'American Patrol' had open cockpits, such heavy clothing was an absolute necessity.

# 46 *Legionnaire 1st Class (Spanish Civil War)*

When the Spanish Civil War began in 1936, the Legion's strength stood at about six 'banderas', each of about 600 men, but before the conflict ended 18 banderas had been raised. This number may be a bit misleading, however, since Italian 'Volunteer' units were sometimes classified as Foreign Legion units. When the war began, the Legion was concentrated in

Morocco. Franco, their former CO, went to Morocco and made sure the Legion was on the Nationalist side. Men of the V Bandera were airlifted to Seville, while some others managed to cross by ship. Later, the Germans supplied Ju-52s to transport large numbers of Legionnaires to the mainland. For the remainder of the war, Legionnaires were used as the Nationalist spearhead, the III, V, and XIII Banderas seeing especially heavy fighting. Perhaps the most famous Legion battle was Badajoz in 1936 where men of the IV and V Banderas led the assault despite very heavy casualties. Legionnaires were involved, though, in virtually every major battle of the war, including the one for Madrid where they clashed with their arch enemies – the International Brigades.

The figure illustrated wears the well-known Legion sidecap with red piping and tassel. The red inverted 'V' on the right side of the cap is the rank insignia for a Legionnaire 1st Class. On the front of his cap is the Legion crest. His light green shirt also carries the Legion crest on the shoulder straps, plus the machine-gunner's insignia on the right breast and rank insignia on the left breast. The trousers are the darker green of the cap, also in typical Legion fashion. His boots are the canvas-topped 'botas alpargatas' worn by the Legion from the 20s through the 50s. The black leather suspenders passing under the shoulder straps have also remained in use with the Legion for decades.

As a machine-gunner, this Legionnaire carries a pistol on his left hip – an M1921 Astra to be exact. The machine-gun is a 7 mm. Hotchkiss M1922 LMG.

# 47 Corporal (early 1930s)

At the end of the Riff War, the Tercio continued to serve in Spanish North Africa, though III, V, and VI Banderas were used in September, 1934, on the mainland to quell an insurrection by Asturian miners. No doubt some of the Republicans' bitter hatred for the Legion stemmed from this episode.

The figure illustrated wears the standard Legion sidecap with corporal's insignia visible on the right side. His uniform was the standard campaign dress during the period 1925–38. His shirt is the standard light green one with Legion insignia on the shoulder straps and rank insignia on the left breast. The jodhpur-style breeches are very distinctive of the Tercio and are especially noteworthy for being bloused at the thighs and closely buttoned over the calves. Note also the strap which passes beneath the 'botas alpergatas'. The cartridge pouches, belt, suspenders, and haversack are all of brown leather. Note that in typical Legion fashion the suspenders pass beneath the shoulder straps. A bayonet was normally worn on the left side. His rifle is the Model 1893 7 mm Mauser.

---

# 48 *Lieutenant, (early 1920s)*

The Spanish Foreign Legion was created in January, 1920. Such an elite unit had been proposed by Millan Astray who as a LTC became the Legion's first commander. Astray created the 'Credo of the Legion', which held that death in combat was the greatest honor. Astray's influence can also be seen in the Legion's battle cry, 'Viva la muerte!' (Long live death!). 'Long live Spain, long live the King, Long live the Legion!' was another battle cry which illustrates the three loyalties, along with a militaristic Catholicism, expected of Legionnaires by Astray.

Unlike the French Foreign Legion which denies Frenchmen the right to serve, Spaniards can serve in the Spanish Foreign Legion, and from the beginning, foreigners have only made up 25 per cent. of the Legion's manpower or less. Harking back to the elite Spanish formations of the Renaissance, Legion regiments (actually nearer to brigades in organization and strength) are known as 'Tercios'. Tercio is also sometimes used as a generic name for the Legion as well. Each 'Tercio' is broken into 'banderas' of about 600 men. The bandera is the unit to which Legionnaires feel their strongest loyalty and which carries their battle honors. When formed, the Legion received better pay than the rest of the Spanish Army and had its pick of the best officers. As Astray, who had studied the French Foreign Legion, had foreseen, the Legion immediately became the elite of the Spanish Army. Astray's second in command was Francisco Franco, who would later command the Legion from 1923–27 and would count on their support throughout his long rule in Spain.

The Riff Rebellion between 1921 and 1926 gave the Legion its baptism of fire, and it rose to the task magnificently, acting as shock troops throughout the war and normally providing the vanguard when advancing and the rearguard when retreating. During the decisive Battle of Alhucemas (1925) Legionnaires provided the spearhead. By the end of the Riff War, Legion strength had grown to eight banderas.

The early Legion officer illustrated wears the Legion side cap with his rank – denoted by the two stars – and the royal crown on the front. As with enlisted personnel, the red tassel is also worn. The dark green tunic is worn over a light green shirt and tie and dark green breeches. Leather gaiters and a leather Sam Browne belt complete the uniform. Both officers and enlisted personnel wore capes, but the enlisted version was much plainer than the officers'. Note the fur collar on this officer's cape and the white silk lining, for example. All ranks wore their rank insignia and the Legion insignia on the left breast of the cape as illustrated. White gloves were also standard for officers.

# 49 *Lieutenant, Condor Legion*

The Condor Legion was sent by Hitler to aid the Nationalists in the Spanish Civil War. It initially comprised about 6500 men in a bomber group, a fighter group, and anti-aircraft, anti-tank, and armored units. Originally, the bomber group was equipped with Ju-52s and the fighter group with He-51s and Me-109s. By the spring of 1938 almost 250 German aircraft in four fighter groups, four bomber groups, and a reconnaissance group; 180 tanks in a tank corps; and 180 37 mm. anti-tank guns in 30 anti-tank companies formed the Condor Legion.

In Spain German officers got a chance to try out tactics such as dive bombing and carpet bombing and to give pilots and tank crews combat experience in Blitzkrieg warfare. The bombing of Guernica immortalized by Picasso will always be remembered as a Condor Legion operation. Among the well-known German officers receiving experience in Spain were Galland and Mölders von Thoma.

So effective was the Condor Legion that the Luftwaffe element was moved from front to front whenever an offensive was planned. To facilitate these moves, the Condor Legion HQ was placed aboard a train so it could be moved rapidly. Some idea of the number of Germans who served in the Condor Legion can be gained from the fact that Hitler reviewed 14,000 veterans of the Legion in Berlin in May 1939.

The figure illustrated is dressed, as were the other veterans for the Berlin parade, in a uniform reportedly converted from a Reichs Arbeitsdienst uniform. On his sidecap and left breast he wears the two stars denoting his rank. The yellow backing indicates his assignment to an aviation unit. Other backings included: blue – medical, red – anti-aircraft, brown – signals, green – administration and supply, and black – staff. The Sam Browne belt and black leather jack boots complete the uniform. On his right breast he wears Spanish aviator's wings and the Spanish Cross, a German award to members of the Condor Legion; on his left, is the Spanish Military Order of Merit.

# 50 Machine-gunner, Abraham Lincoln Battalion

Around 40,000 foreigners — mostly Socialists — fought in the various International Brigades at various times during the war, though the maximum number in the Brigades at any one time was 18,000. Frequently, the International Brigades were used as shock troops and accordingly suffered heavy casualties. The International Brigades and the Spanish Foreign Legion, Republican and Nationalist elite troops respectively, fought especially bitterly against each other when they met. During the Spanish Civil War about 3000 Americans fought for the Republicans. The Abraham Lincoln Battalion was the most famous American formation, though there was also a George Washington Battalion and a John Brown Artillery Battery. International battalions were not entirely American, however. At various times Englishmen, Scots, Welshmen, Irishmen, and Canadians, among others, formed significant portions of the 'American' battalions. In fact, by late in the war, the International Brigades had all become predominantly Spanish in composition. The 450 strong Abraham Lincoln Battalion first saw action in the Battle of Jarama on 17 February 1937 where they suffered 295 casualties. Losses among the American battalions were so heavy at Brunete in July, 1937, that they were merged into one. Well over 2000 Americans were killed or wounded fighting in the International Brigades. Later, 600 veterans of the International Brigades would serve in the US armed forces during World War II. Interestingly enough, seven of them served with the OSS. A few of the British survivors were recruited into the SAS in the Western Desert in 1941.

The figure illustrated wears what might be termed the 'uniform' of the Abraham Lincoln Battalion, though generally the International Brigades wore a somewhat motley assortment of uniform items. The blue flannel shirt was, however, fairly widely worn in the Abraham Lincoln Battalion as were the brown breeches with puttees. The sidecap and webbed gear are US World War I issue and were also somewhat standardized among the Americans.

As a secondary weapon, this figure carries a 9 mm Astra M1921 pistol tucked into his webbed belt. His primary weapon is the Soviet DP 7.62 mm. squad automatic weapon equipped with a 47-round drum magazine. The normal rifle issued to members of the Abraham Lincoln Battalion was the M1891 Mosin-Nagant.

# 51 Tanker, Italian Volunteer

By mid-1937 the Italian 'Corpo Truppe Volontaire' numbered 50,000 men serving in Spain with the Nationalists. As many as 6000 Italians were killed fighting for the Nationalists. At various times, Italians were assigned to the Spanish Foreign Legion and to mixed Italian/Spanish units. However, there were also entire Italian divisions which were sent as 'volunteers', including the Littorio Division and the March 23 Division, the latter composed of staunch Fascists from the Black Shirts. Included among the Italian forces were two tank battalions equipped with L3s.

The 'Carrista' illustrated wears the operational uniform consisting of a leather crash helmet and leather three quarter length, double-breasted coat worn over a gray-green tunic and breeches. The leather gaiters have a distinctive long strap which wraps around them and then buckles.

# 52 1st Lieutenant, Kosciusko Squadron

The Polish War of Independence (February 1919–October

1920) attracted a small group of American aviators to the Polish cause. Recruited by Captain Merian Cooper, 17 Americans eventually served in the Kosciusko Squadron, which was named after the Polish patriot who had fought for the United States during the American Revolution. Cooper's first recruit was Major Cedric Fauntleroy whom he had known in the American Air Service. Fauntleroy would soon take over from a Polish officer as CO of the Kosciusko Squadron. The first American aviators arrived in Poland in October 1919. Their original contract called for them to serve for six months at the same rates of pay and with the same status as Polish officers. Normally, each officer entered at the rank he had held in his own country's air service. One final interesting note on Merian Cooper is that he later served for a short time on Chennault's staff with the Flying Tigers. For millions of movie fans, however, Cooper's fame will rest not on his adventures with the Kosciusko Squadron or the Flying Tigers but on the fact he produced the movie *King Kong*.

Of the original ten recruits (seven more joined later), five had served in the British or French air service during World War I, thus indicating they already had a bent as soldiers of fortune. The other five had flown for the American Air Service. The new recruits joined the Polish 7th Fighter Squadron, which became the Kosciusko Squadron under Major Fauntleroy, though a few Polish officers and the Polish groundcrewmen remained with the squadron. Originally, the unit was equipped with Albatros D.IIIs which were later replaced by Italian Balilla fighters in July 1920. One American officer, Kenneth Murray, had his own Sopwith Camel shipped from the States for him to fly. The squadron was organized into two flights — the 'Pulaski' (named after another Pole who had served during the American Revolution and who when mortally wounded had supposedly been helped from the battlefield by an ancestor of Merian Cooper's), whose aircraft had red-painted noses, and the 'Kosciusko' flight, whose aircraft had blue-painted noses. During the war, the 7th Fighter Squadron flew 659 sorties, but about one-half of these were flown before the arrival of the Americans. It is probable that the Americans flew between 300 and 400 sorties, though it is possible they flew many more. The Kosciusko Squadron certainly played an important role during the Polish retreat from Kiev as they acted as an aerial rearguard, attacking Cossack cavalry units constantly from the air so that they could not harry the retreating Poles. After the war ended, the remaining members of the Kosciusko Squadron were demobilized on 15 May 1921.

The figure illustrated wears the 'rogatywka', the traditional Polish four-sided hat with the Polish eagle hat badge. The two silver stars designate 1st lieutenant's rank. Earlier, rank had been denoted on the hat by a disk bearing bars, and two silver bars would have designated 1st lieutenant's rank. The Haller or 'lake' blue uniform was standard for Polish officers. Sam Browne belt and soft leather boots are worn by this officer.

On his right breast he wears the badge of the Kosciusko Squadron, which was also painted on squadron aircraft. It consisted of a circular badge surrounded by 13 stars and having 13 vertical stripes. To give the impression of red and white stripes, the disk was pierced and normally backed with a red ribbon. Superimposed on the disc is the 'rogatywka' and crossed scythes, the latter associated with the peasant's revolt Kosciusko had led when he returned from America. On his upper left breast this figure wears the diving eagle Polish aviator's wings. The medals on his left breast are: Virtuti Militari, V Class; Cross of Valor; Haller Medal; and Cross of the Polish Soldiers from America. The latter two were awarded to all members of the squadron.

# 53 *2nd Lieutenant, Escadrille Lafayette*

During World War I more than 200 Americans flew for France, many being sent into combat after only 50 hours of flight training. By 1916 it had been decided to form a squadron entirely of Americans. This unit was originally known as the 'Escadrille Americaine', but because of German pressure on the American government about this 'breach of neutrality', the name was changed to 'Escadrille Lafayette'. Though only 38 Americans actually flew for the unit, there is a tendency to lump all American aviators flying for France under this title. This is incorrect. 'Lafayette Flying Corps' is normally the generic term given to all of the American aviators in the Service Aéronautique. It should be understood, then, that the Escadrille Lafayette was a specific squadron – N-124. The squadron insignia was also distinctively American, bearing the head of an Indian chief. Among the more well-known of the Escadrille Lafayette fliers were Raoul Lufberry (upon whom the figure illustrated is based) and James Norman Hall, later to achieve fame as the co-author of *Mutiny on the Bounty*. On 18 February 1918, the Escadrille Lafayette was incorporated into the US Air Service as the 103rd Aero Squadron, though many of the veteran fliers were given commands of other American squadrons where their combat experience could be put to good use. Those Americans flying for France, both within the Escadrille Lafayette and without, ended up scoring 199 aerial victories.

The pilot illustrated wears a képi with blue-gray tunic and breeches. Leather gaiters are also worn. His collar badges are the winged, five-pointed stars worn by French aviators. French pilot's wings are worn on the right breast, and on the left breast he wears the Legion of Honour, Médaille Militaire, and Croix de Guerre. At his feet is Whiskey, one of the Escadrille Lafayette's mascots.

For actual flying, especially in the winter, the pilots wore heavy, fur-lined clothing in the unheated cockpits.

# 54 *Flying Officer, RAF Eagle Squadrons*

Between 1940 and 1941 approximately 240 U.S. pilots were enlisted into the RAF. Many of these fliers were recruited in the USA by an archetypal soldier of fortune named Charles Sweeney, who had served in the French Foreign Legion in World War I, been a brigadier general for the Poles during the Russo–Polish War, organized a squadron of pilots who flew for the French during the Riff War, served as the chief of the Sultan of Morocco's Air Force, and fought for the Republicans in Spain. The men recruited by Sweeney were supposed to be experienced pilots, though many exaggerated their flying hours to get accepted. Eventually, one in three of the men recruited would be killed in action or killed on active service (i.e. crashes, etc.).

The first Eagle Squadron – 71 Squadron – was activated in 1940 and was followed by two others – 121 and 133 Squadrons. Originally, the Eagle Squadrons were equipped with Hurricanes, but in August 1941, 71 Squadron received Spitfires. In October, 1941, 121 and 133 Squadrons also received Spitfires. Although the Eagle Squadrons flew from bases in the UK, some pilots volunteered to serve in Malta where they saw a great deal of action. In September 1942, the Eagle Squadrons were transferred to the USAAF where they became the 4th Fighter Group. Because of their combat experience, however, many members of the Eagle Squadrons were given command positions in the USAAF.

Members of the Eagle Squadrons were credited with shooting down $73\frac{1}{2}$ enemy planes, though Americans serving with other RAF squadrons probably accounted for at least an equal number of aircraft. The leading American ace with the RAF, in fact, did not fly with the Eagle Squadrons. Lance Wade, who downed 25 enemy aircraft, served with the Desert Air Force. Among those becoming aces with the Eagle Squadrons were Carroll McColpin (eight victories), Chesley

Peterson (six victories with the Eagle Squadrons and one with the USAAF), Reade Tilley (seven victories), Gregory Daymond (seven victories), and William Dunn (five victories with the Eagle Squadrons and one with the USAAF). In all there were twenty American aces in the RAF.

The pilot illustrated wears the Type C General Purpose Flying Helmet with goggles and anti glare lenses. Radio and oxygen plugs are visible dangling from the mask. His uniform is the standard RAF blue-gray tunic and trousers, worn over a 'turtle neck' sweater. His flying boots are the 1940 pattern with canvas upper portions. Over his tunic he wears a life vest. On his left shoulder he wears the Eagle Squadron insignia. His rank – flying officer – is indicated by the medium blue line of braid and two narrow lines of black braid on his cuff. Rank would also be worn on the shoulder straps, though in this illustration the life vest obscures them. Also worn on this uniform but not visible because of the life jacket are RAF pilot's wings on his left breast. After incorporation into the USAAF, former members of the Eagle Squadrons normally wore their RAF wings on the right breast and their USAAF wings on the left breast.

## 55 Lieutenant, Spanish Blue Division, Russia

In return for assistance to the Nationalists during the Spanish Civil War and out of hatred for the Russian Communists (who had supported the Republicans in the Spanish Civil War), the Spanish Falangist government raised a volunteer division to serve with the Wehrmacht on the Eastern Front. This 18,000 strong division was officially the Spanish Volunteer Division, but because of the blue Falangist shirts worn by its members, it was often known as the 'Blue Division'.

On 25 July 1941 the Spanish volunteers entered the Wehrmacht as the 250th Infantry Division, and by October the division was in combat in Russia. During the next two years, the Blue Division fought courageously, taking part in the siege of Leningrad and the Battle of Krasny Bor among other actions. By the time the division was repatriated to Spain it had suffered over 12,000 casualties, including about 4000 killed. Replacements had periodically arrived from Spain, and some veterans had been rotated home. A smaller Spanish Legion of about 1500 volunteers continued to fight until April 1944, when they were sent home to Spain as well. Spanish volunteers also served in the Luftwaffe in the 'Blue Squadron'.

The figure illustrated wears a field-gray peaked cap with German eagle and cockade, and a field-gray tunic and breeches with boots. The blue Falangist shirt is worn under the tunic with the collars out in a style favored by many members of the Blue Division. His shoulder boards bear the single 'pip' of a lieutenant and the yellow 'Waffenfarbe' indicating he is a member of the division's reconnaissance group. The yellow Waffenfarbe is also worn on the collar insignia. On his right sleeve is the arm shield worn by the Spanish volunteers. The Wehrmacht eagle is on the right breast. The ribbon of the Iron Cross, 2nd Class is worn at his button-hole. On the left breast are his Spanish ribbons, including the Order of Military Merit, and the Falangist badge. German awards on the left breast include an infantry assault badge and a wound badge. His pistol is a P08 Luger.

---

## 56 Sturmmann, 13th Waffen-Gibirgs-Division der SS 'Handschar'

As the Waffen SS began to lower its racial standards in an attempt to increase the number of divisions in the field, one source it tapped was the Moslems living in Bosnia and Herzegovina. As a result, the 'Handschar' division was formed from these Croatians in March 1943. Himmler actually liked the idea of recruiting Moslems since their religion taught that dying in battle assured one he would go to heaven and this – to Himmler's way of thinking – seemed a good religion for a soldier.

The 'Handschar' was used in Yugoslavia for anti-partisan duties. Early in 1944 the division reached a strength of 21,065, but by late in that year many of the Moslem members of the division had been discharged as the Germans pulled out of Bosnia. After the war some members of the division, both Germans and Moslems, were tried for war crimes since the anti-partisan fighting had been especially brutal.

The most noteworthy aspect of the 'Handschar' uniform was the fez, in the case of this figure the field-gray version with a black tassel, was worn for parade and walking-out. An autumn pattern SS camo smock worn over the field gray service tunic and baggy field-gray mountain trousers gathered with elastic puttees over mountain boots complete the basic uniform. On the right collar patch is worn the divisional insignia and on the left collar patch the rank insignia for an SS Sturmmann.

Affixed to his webbed equipment he carries the standard M1935 steel helmet. Tucked into his belt is an StG39 grenade, and on his left hip he wears a triple magazine pouch for the MP40 SMG, which is slung over his left shoulder.

# 57 *Free India Legionnaire*

Indian Nationalists Mohan Singh and his successor Subhas Chandra Bose recruited troops for the Japanese and Germans from among Indian Army POWs. Two understrength Indian National Army divisions were raised for the Japanese and were used in the CBI Theater, though they did not prove very effective. Those Indians recruited for the Germans, primarily from POWs taken in North Africa, formed the Free India Legion (Infantry-Regiment 950) which at its peak comprised three battalions totalling about 2000 men. The Legion was originally offered to Rommel for use in North Africa, but he refused. In 1943, the Legion was ordered to Holland but mutinied and were sent to southwestern France instead. In 1944 they were accused of atrocities in the Bordeaux area.

This figure wears the traditional pagris as his head gear. His tunic is the tropical field service pattern, worn open at the neck over a shirt and tie. Trousers are also tropical service pattern. On his right upper sleeve is the shield of the Free India Legion. His collar patches and shoulder straps bear the white Waffenfarbe of the infantry. The Wehrmacht eagle is on his right breast. His belt is the standard Wehrmacht enlisted man's pattern.

# 58 *Flying Tiger*

The American Volunteer Group – commonly known as the 'Flying Tigers' – was formed in April 1941, when Claire Chennault was empowered by Chiang Kai-shek to recruit pilots and groundcrewmen to fly and maintain the 100 P-40 fighters China was purchasing from the USA to use in her war against Japan. Contracts to serve in China were issued through CAMCO (Central Aircraft Manufacturing Company), China's 'agent' for handling the purchase of the aircraft and the hiring of personnel. Salaries of $250–$750 per month plus travel and allowances, housing, 30 days' paid leave, and a $500 bonus to pilots for each enemy aircraft shot down were offered. Later, after the AVG became operational, bonuses would be extended to include enemy planes destroyed on the ground. In all, 109 pilots and 190 groundcrewmen were recruited.

Chennault proved a perfect leader for the soldiers of fortune who comprised the AVG. Chennault's tactical methods, taught to new AVG members in 72 classroom hours and 60 flying hours, also proved sound as he trained the pilots to attack in pairs and to use the P-40's advantages – sturdiness, firepower, and diving power. Included in his classroom lectures were simple and easy to remember diagrams of Japanese aircraft with vulnerable points marked in brightly colored chalk. Many AVG members later found themselves attacking and instinctively firing accurately at vulnerable points as a result of this training. Chennault trained his fliers to 'make a pass, shoot and break away'.

The AVG was divided into three squadrons – the Adam-and-Eves, Panda Bears, and Hell's Angels. The Flying Tigers took part in the defense of Rangoon in conjunction with British fliers, but their fame was won over China. The AVG was disbanded in July 1942, but in only seven months of combat flying had established an impressive record. The Flying Tigers were credited with shooting down at least 299 enemy planes, with another 153 probables. More than 200 enemy planes had been destroyed on the ground as well. Twenty-nine Tigers became aces flying with the AVG, with Bob Neale ($15\frac{1}{2}$ victories) and 'Tex' Hill ($12\frac{1}{2}$ victories) the top scorers. Many other Tigers went on to achieve fame flying with the Navy, Marine Corps, or Army Air Corps. The most famous of these was probably Greg 'Pappy' Boyington, who had scored six victories with the AVG and went on to add another 22 as a Marine aviator in the Pacific war and leader of the renowned Black Sheep Squadron.

Perhaps the most important service performed by the Flying Tigers, though, was the boost they gave to American morale in the dark days after Pearl Harbor, when the only American victories anywhere in the world were those of the Flying Tigers.

The Tiger illustrated wears a light bush jacket and trousers of the type purchased by some members of the AVG in the Far East. His overseas cap bears Chinese officers cap badge. On the right collar are the initials A.V.G. and on the left collar is a US-style aviator's collar insignia. The Flying Tiger pin is worn on the right breast and Chinese aviator's wings are worn on the left breast. The AVG shoulder sleeve insignia is on the left sleeve.

# 59 *Flying Tiger*

The figure illustrated is dressed for a mission. His helmet is standard US military type, and his flight suit is US Navy issue, these being purchased from the Navy by China and issued to the AVG. His flight jacket is also US Navy pattern, part of the same Chinese purchase. A leather AVG patch is worn over the left breast. The silk scarf, which bears Chiang Kai-shek's chop, was a Christmas gift from the Generalissimo to members of the Flying Tigers.

The pistol being cocked by this pilot is the Colt Model 1908 .380 auto, a popular choice among the Tigers, each of whom furnished his own personal sidearm.

# 60 *Flying Tiger*

This pilot on the way to the flight line wears the officer's peaked cap with Chinese officer's cap badge. His flight jacket is the heavy fleece-lined type popular with many of the Flying Tigers. (Army A-2 flight jackets were also worn.) On the back of the jacket is the famous 'blood chit', which guaranteed a reward to any Chinese helping a downed Tiger. A flying coverall is worn beneath the jacket. In his left hand this figure carries a Chinese parachute bag.

# 61 *Legionnaire, 3rd REI, Algeria (c.1960)*

The war in Algeria ran from 1954 until 1962, and during that period the bulk of the fighting was borne by the Legion and the colonial paras. In the process, the Legion suffered almost 2000 men killed. It was a brutal war on both sides and the Legionnaires ruthlessly crushed the ALN (Armée de Libération Nationale) and the FLN (Front de Libération Nationale) both in the cities and in the 'bled'. At El Halia in August 1955, for example, the ALN slaughtered 71 Europeans. In retaliation, Legionnaires killed over 1200 Algerians. As with any counter-insurgency war, the atrocities committed by the 'liberation movement' tended to be ignored by the leftist press, while Legion reprisals drew atrocity headlines. The fact that many Legionnaires were Germans only added to claims of neo-Fascist suppression.

Under Gen. Maurice Challe, Legionnaires and paras were used as reserve 'intervention' units who were sent in to eliminate ALN units once they had been 'fixed' by other units. Despite the success on the battlefield, a political settlement calling for a French pullout resulted in the 'Putsch' of April, 1960. One Legion unit – the famous 1st REP (Régiment Étrangère de Parachutistes) – was the key military unit in the abortive revolt, and, as a result, was disbanded. Among the Legion units which served in Algeria during the war were the following: 1st RE, 2nd REI, 3rd REI, 4th REI, 5th REI, 13th DBLE, 1st REC, 2nd REC, 1st REP, and 2nd REP.

The Legionnaire illustrated wears the green beret with the infantry beret badge consisting of a grenade bearing the regimental number. He wears the later pattern 'lizard' camo infantry utilities with black combat boots. Only basic webbed gear consisting of pistol, belt, suspenders, magazine pouches, and canteen is worn. The position of his left hand and the ready position of his MAT-49 SMG indicate that he is probably manning a roadblock.

# 62 Sergent-chef, 1st BEP, Indochina (c.1951)

Along with the Colonial paratroops, the Legion bore the brunt of combat in the Indochina War. The 2nd REI, 3rd REI, 5th REI, 13th DBLE, 1st REC, 1st BEP, and 2nd BEP all saw action during the war, with the two parachute battalions seeing especially heavy combat. The 1st BEP (Bataillon Étranger de Parachutistes) arrived in Indochina late in 1948 and was virtually wiped out during the retreat from the Cao Bang Ridgeline late in 1950. Re-formed in March, 1951, the 1st BEP saw heavy action for the next $2\frac{1}{2}$ years, and in November, 1953, jumped at Dien Bien Phu where the unit was again virtually wiped out when that fortress fell. Members of the 1st BEP participated in at least 12 combat jumps during the Indochina War.

The para illustrated wears the khaki bush hat, which was widely used by French forces throughout the Indochina War. His camouflage jacket is the US World War II Pacific Theater pattern. As was often the practice in the 1st BEP it is worn with the French green utility trousers. Brown French jump boots are worn. On the sleeve of the camo jacket are the three chevrons of a sergent-chef and the Legion écusson.

Webbed gear is of US pattern and on the pistol belt carries pouches for 15-round M1 Carbine magazines. The weapon is the US M1A1 paratrooper's version of the M1 Carbine.

# 63 Caporal, 13th DBLE, Bir Hakeim, World War II

Various Legion units fought during the Battle for France, but after France's surrender, most were either disbanded or sent to the Vichy-controlled colonies in North Africa. The primary Legion unit which continued to fight for the allies as part of the Free French Brigade was the 13th DBLE (Demi-Brigade de la Légion Étrangère). This unit fought throughout the North

African campaign as part of the British 8th Army. It is the 13th DBLE which is remembered for its heroic defense of Bir Hakeim and for its part in the Battle of El Alamein. As part of the 1st Free French Division, the 13th DBLE later fought in Italy and France itself.

The figure illustrated wears a much-used white képi. Despite the fact that these képis virtually fell apart from wear, as many Legionnaires as possible retained them throughout the war. His British battle dress jacket is worn over British shorts. The boots and anklets are also British. On the battle dress jacket he wears a green Legion grenade on each collar patch and corporal's chevron over the Free French Cross of Lorraine insignia on his right sleeve. His leather equipment is the French 1935 pattern as is his canteen. His rifle is the MAS 1936.

---

# 64 Gurkha Rifleman, Malaya (c.1957)

In 1947 when India and Pakistan were granted their independence, the 2nd King Edward VII's Own Gurkhas (the Sirmoor Rifles), 6th Gurkha Rifles (later 6th Queen Elizabeth's Own Gurkha Rifles), 7th Gurkha Rifles (later 7th Duke of Edinburgh's Own Gurkha Rifles), and 10th Gurkha Rifles (later 10th Princess Mary's Own Gurkha Rifles) stayed with the British Army, while the remaining six Gurkha regiments became part of the Indian Army. By 1948 when the Malayan Emergency began, all four Gurkha regiments were serving in Malaya, though many battalions contained a large number of recruits to bring them back up to strength since members of those regiments joining the British Army had had the option of transferring to the Indian Army and some had done so.

For the next ten years battalions of the Gurkha regiments would be serving in Malaya with each battalion periodically being rotated out of combat to duty in Hong Kong. Early in the Malayan Emergency Gurkhas had served in Ferret Force, which had been especially trained in jungle operations. Throughout the emergency the Gurkhas patrolled and fought with their usual tenacity, and they proved especially skilled at setting ambushes for the Communist terrorists driven towards them by SAS deep penetration patrols.

The rifleman illustrated wears the jungle hat, which often had a colored band or some other type of field sign so that its wearer could be recognized and not mistaken for the enemy. Such recognition signs were especially important for the Gurkhas in Malaya and Borneo since the enemy also had Oriental features. The uniform consists of the 'jungle greens' widely worn in Malaya. Canvas and rubber jungle boots are worn with puttees and ties on the trousers to give added protection from leeches.

The '44 pattern webbed equipment is worn, but note that for more comfort in the jungle the ammunition pouches are worn on the belt at the hip rather than in the standard position. The sheath for the kukri is visible behind the right leg, though the actual blade is in his hand. The self-loading rifle is the 7.62 mm L1A1, which entered service in 1954.

## 65 Gurkha Rifleman, 4th Indian Division, World War II

During World War II nearly 250,000 Gurkhas served in the ten Gurkha regiments, some of which were expanded to four or five battalions during the war, or in the two new regiments – the 25th and 26th – raised for the war. Gurkha battalions served in the Far East, Middle East, North Africa, Italy, and Greece. The Gurkhas played an especially important part in the fighting in Burma under General Slim, a former Gurkha officer, and operating with the Chindits. In Europe, the Gurkhas, being highlanders, proved especially valuable in the Italian Campaign where many Gurkha battalions fought heroically in the Battle for Monte Cassino.

The figure illustrated wears the British Mark I helmet with net cover. His uniform is the serge battle dress adopted in 1939. On his left shoulder he wears the divisional insignia for the 4th Indian Division, probably indicating that he is in the 1/2 or 2/7 Gurkha Rifles since these battalions served with the 4th Indian Division throughout much of the war. Over his ankle length boots he wears anklets. His webbed equipment is the 1937 pattern with the addition of the kukri behind his right hip. His SMG is the M1928 Thompson.

## 66 Rifleman, 2/7 Duke of Edinburgh's Own Gurkha Rifles, Hong Kong (1982)

The 2nd Battalion of the 7th Duke of Edinburgh's Own Gurkha Rifles was recently re-formed for security duties in Hong Kong. Unlike other Gurkha battalions, the 2/7 was formed as a mixed battalion, with soldiers drawn from both eastern and western Nepal. Normally, since World War II, Gurkha battalions have been drawn entirely from the same part of Nepal. Since it was formed primarily for border patrol and security duties in Hong Kong, the 2/7 has a strength of only about two-thirds that of a normal battalion, lacking heavy weapons, mortar, anti-tank, and engineer elements. One of the principal missions of the 2/7 is to provide security along the border with China to prevent illegal immigrants from entering the Crown Colony.

The Gurkha illustrated is dressed for border security duties in support of the Hong Kong police. He wears a jungle hat with the DPM tropical jacket and trousers. His boots, DMS (direct molded soles) are worn with puttees. His equipment consists of only a pistol belt with canteen and the kukri. The kukri is the traditional utility/fighting knife and chopping implement of the Gurkhas and is normally about 16 inches in overall length. Its heavy, curved, single-edged blade is about 12 inches in length and is balanced and designed so that it can be wielded with great power. There are many instances of Gurkhas either decapitating an enemy or cleaving through his head and into his chest with one blow of the kukri. In lieu of an L1A1 a riot baton/staff is carried to deal with any illegal immigrants who should become recalcitrant. One final noteworthy item for anyone who has served in Hong Kong or done R & R there is this Gurkha's Seiko watch, an item few leave Hong Kong without purchasing unless they already possess a Hever or a Rolex!

# 67 *Nung, SOG Recon Team (c.1970)*

The Nungs were an ethnic Chinese tribe originally from the border area between North Vietnam and China. Nungs had served in their own units under the French and had been among the best indigenous troops in Indochina. Because of their fighting ability and loyalty to the Americans (who it should be noted paid them very well), the Nungs were usually the most reliable elements in the various irregular forces formed by the US Special Forces. Nungs were used as bodyguards for Special Forces personnel and as guard detachments for Special Forces installations. They also formed a large proportion of the elite MIKE Force strike units. Clandestine recon and raiding units such as MACV/SOG (Military Assistance Command Vietnam/Studies and Observations Group) relied heavily on Nungs, too. It should be noted, by the way, that true Nungs, who had a long heritage as warriors, should not be confused with the 'Cholon Cowboys' from Saigon who claimed to be Nungs.

The Nung illustrated is a member of a SOG Recon Team preparing for a mission. He wears an OD cloth head scarf and tiger striped camo utilities. US jungle boots are his footwear.

His webbed gear is the STABO rig which was designed for Special Forces operations and which allowed its wearer to be extracted via helicopter while still keeping both hands free to fire his weapon. Note that the straps of the harness which would pass under the thighs during an extraction hang loose for comfort. The fighting/survival knife is carried on the suspender in typical recon team fashion. His weapon is the XM177E2. Before leaving on the patrol, for good luck, this Nung is lighting a joss stick which he has tied to his weapon.

---

# 68 *Montagnard 'Striker' (c.1965)*

'Montagnard' is a French term meaning mountain men and was used to refer to the tribes living in the highlands of Vietnam. The Vietnamese called the Montagnards the 'moi', which meant savages, and there was great animosity between the 'Yards' and the 'Viets'. Although the Montagnards were not traditionally mercenary soldiers as were the Nungs, there were Yards who were paid professionals. The French GCMA (Groupement de Commandos Mixtes Aéroportés) – equivalent to the US Special Forces – had formed irregular units from among the Montagnards during the Indochina War, and so did the Special Forces during the Vietnam War.

Many of the Montagnards were formed into unpaid local militia units as part of the CIDG (Civilian Irregular Defense Group) program. Some of the younger men who showed good military potential, however, were formed into professional 'strike forces'. These strikers, along with some Yards who later served with the SOG Recon Teams and the MIKE Forces, were true professional elements.

The striker illustrated wears the 'duck hunter' camo pattern utility hat, jacket, and trousers issued to SF trained irregulars during the mid-1960s. His shoes are the 'Bata boots' popular with the indigenous troops and some US advisors. An M26A1 fragmentation grenade is worn on the suspenders, and his weapon is an M3 'Grease Gun'. Spare 30-round magazines for the M3 are carried in the pouch on his left hip.

# 69 *Air America Pilot*

Air America was the CIA-owned airline which carried out all sorts of missions during the Vietnam War. Air America's motto was, 'Anything, Anywhere, Anytime – Professionally', and the company lived up to that motto. Agent insertions or extractions, guerrilla support operations, 'hard rice' (arms) drops, U-2 reconnaissance flights – Air America carried them all out. Though Air America is often used generically for all of the CIA-owned air assets, there were others such as Air Asia, Continental Air Services, Southern Air Transport, et. al. operating in Laos and elsewhere in Southeast Asia.

Air America was so large at its peak that it was the largest airline in the free world, and some say in the entire world. No one was really sure how many planes and personnel were involved because of the cloak of secrecy surrounding the operation which fell under the Directorate for Plans (a.k.a. 'Dirty Tricks Department'). Not only was Air America large but it was profitable, thus giving the CIA a source of additional funds. Though Air America flew everything from helicopters to 727s and U-2s, the planes most associated with AA in Vietnam and Laos may have been the STOL aircraft such as the Helio-Courier, which could land in as little as 75 feet, or its successor the Pilatus Porter. Air America continued to operate in Southeast Asia until the fall of Saigon, during which AA pilots played a heroic part in the evacuation.

The figure illustrated wears the gray peaked cap, light gray shirt, and darker gray trousers which were closest to a standard uniform worn by AA pilots. Baseball caps and stetsons often replaced the peaked cap and coveralls were often worn while flying. The AA cap badge and pilot's wings were unique to Air America, however. Indicative of the casual attitude about attire among AA personnel are the cowboy boots worn by this pilot.

Aviator's sun glasses, Rolex watch, and gold link bracelet – the latter for 'buying his way out' should he crash – were all very typical of AA pilots. Originally, AA pilots were prohibited from carrying weapons, but after some downed pilots were executed by the enemy, this rule was relaxed and most started carrying some type of armament while flying. In this case, a S & W .38 Special revolver is carried in a Berns Martin 'Lightning' shoulder holster.

In his left hand is the AA 'Flight Information Pamphlet', which contained information about airfields likely to be used (along with a few very unlikely ones), call signs, emergency procedures, and code names. Nationality codes, for example, were: Vietnamese – white, Chinese – green, Filipino – orange, American – purple, Australian – blue, and unknown – black. Status codes were: military – tree, embassy employee – sand, USAID employee – river, Air America employee – mountain, and civilian, no connection, or unknown – lake.

# 70 Spanish Foreign Legion Lieutenant (c.1965)

During the 1950s and 1960s, the Spanish Foreign Legion was used primarily as a colonial force in North Africa where it garrisoned the Spanish enclaves in Morocco and the Spanish Sahara. In the Spanish Sahara, the Legionnaires saw combat against Moroccan irregulars during the later 1950s, with the most famous action probably taking place at Edchera in January, 1958. The 1960s also saw the influx into the Legion of a few of the mercenary veterans of the Congo. (Mike Hoare's physical training officer in the Congo, it should be noted, had been a veteran of the Spanish Foreign Legion.) The year 1961 also marked the establishment of an elite within an elite when a Spanish Foreign Legion Parachute Battalion – 'Cabelleros Legionarios Paracaidistas' – was established.

The officer illustrated wears the traditional Legion officer's green peaked hat. Over a green tunic and riding breeches, he wears the dark green, trench-style raincoat. The two stars denoting lieutenant's rank and the Legion crest are worn on the shoulder straps, and branch insignia are worn on the collars. The shirt and tie are both green as well. The white gloves and black riding boots complete this officer's uniform.

# 71 *Legionnaire, Sahara (c.1975)*

During the late 1960s and early 1970s, Spain began to divest itself of the remains of its colonies as Morocco assumed control of Ifni in 1969 and the Spanish Sahara was ceded to Morocco and Mauretania in 1976. Some 5000 or more Legionnaires remained, however, at Cueta and Melilla – two small enclaves in Morocco – and in the Canary Islands. As of 1979, Legion strength stood at about 10,000.

The figure illustrated wears the regulation uniform for duty in the Sahara. The green utility cap is covered by a long neck flap, which is also used to protect the face from the sun or sandstorms. Sand goggles are worn over this cover. A light green shirt is worn with darker green shorts and light green long stockings. Issue sandals provide the footwear. Note that on the right shirt pocket this Legionnaire wears a unit pocket crest on a fob, in this case for 'Del Grupo Ligero Saharjano I'. The black leather belt supported by suspenders has a plate over the buckle bearing the Legion crest. Leather magazine pouches are worn on the left and right hips. The weapon is the Spanish M58 CETME 7.62 mm assault rifle.

# 72 Gastadore, VI Bandara (c.1950)

In the Spanish Foreign Legion the Gastadores hold a position somewhat analogous on ceremonial occasions to the French Foreign Legion 'Pioniers'. The gastadore is also a pioneer and just as the French Foreign Legion 'Pioniers' parade with an ax on ceremonial occasions, the Gastadores will often have a saw or another implement, though they also retain their rifle or sub-machine-gun.

The gastadore illustrated wears the standard Legion side cap with red piping and tassel and Legion insignia on the front. The light green shirt with insignia on the shoulder straps and dark green trousers are also standard Legion uniform items. On the left pocket can be seen rank insignia for a 'cabo' (corporal). The boots are the soft black leather 'botos' worn by members of the Legion through the 1950s. The black leather belt and suspenders are also standard items. The plate covering the belt buckle bears the Legion insignia.

Particularly noteworthy among the 'gala' (parade) items are the gauntlets which bear the Legion insignia. At the time of this figure, the gastadores from all Bandaras wore black gauntlets, but more recently the gauntlets have been of the same color as the fourragère. (i.e. black – I Bandara, red – II Bandara, navy – III Bandara, yellow – V Bandara, blue – VI Bandara, white – VII Bandara, and red and white – VIII Bandara.) The blue braided fourragère, the black leather, 'bandolera' with Legion crest, and the shoulder insignia with blue background complete the 'gala' distinctions.

This gastadore's weapon is the Model 1943 7.92 Mauser rifle.

139

# 73 *Major Mike Hoare*

Mike Hoare was born in Dublin and served in World War II with the British Army, reaching the rank of major in the Royal Armored Corps. According to some sources, Hoare also served with the Chindits. Since he served in India and Burma this is quite possible. After the war he emigrated to South Africa where he worked as an accountant, an automobile dealer, and a safari organizer until being hired by Moise Tshombe as a mercenary in Katanga. In 1964, Tshombe called Hoare back to the Congo to organize a mercenary 'Commando' unit to help stiffen the government forces and to carry out special missions.

Hoare formed and trained 5 Commando into an elite strike force of about 200 white mercenaries. His air support was provided by Cuban mercenary pilots flying T-28s and B-26s. Hoare proved a good leader of mercenary troops, knowing when to insist on discipline and when to look the other way. No. 5 Commando acted as a spearhead in virtually every important operation during the 'Simba Revolt', including the advance on Stanleyville.

More recently Hoare led the abortive attempt by a group of mercenaries posing as a rugby team to take over the Seychelles Islands in 1981.

The green beret and shoulder slides are probably Belgian in inspiration. At least some of Hoare's 5 Commando members fabricated their shoulder slides from the covering of the Indian Embassy's billiard table. The commando dagger on the shoulder slides is typically Belgian since this is the insignia used by Belgium to identify commando units. Major's rank, though Hoare was promoted to LTC while in the Congo, on the shoulder slides is also Belgian in style. The khaki battledress was relatively standard for 5 Commando. Hoare wears British-pattern boots and anklets. His weapon, worn on the left hip, is an FN 9 mm. GP35.

The famous 'Wild Geese' shoulder insignia is not being worn

in this illustration, though its choice certainly reflects Hoare's Irish origins.

# 74  *'Colonel' Bob Denard*

Bob Denard is the classic French mercenary. He first turned up fighting for Tshombe in Katanga in 1960. Next, he was in the Yemen leading the French mercenaries fighting for the Royalists there. In 1964 he was back in the Congo commanding the 'Premier Choc'. During the next decade Denard turned up leading his own band of mercenaries – 'les affreux' – in various parts of Africa. In the mid-1970s some of Denard's men were in Angola, though he was not there himself. In January, 1977, Denard led an unsuccessful attempt to take over Benin, a former French colony. His next operation, however, was much more successful. On 13 May 1978, Denard fulfilled the dream of mercenary captains throughout history; he took over his own country – the Comoro Islands. After leaving the Comoros, at least partially at the urging of the French government, Denard gave up 'le baroud' (the mercenary life) to enter retirement, though whether he will stay retired is yet to be seen.

Denard is illustrated in his 'uniform' as chief of police and commandant of the Comoro Army. The green beret of the French Foreign Legion is a staple with French mercenaries, though Denard does not wear the Legion beret badge. The shirt is a very light blue/white and bears the French para's brevet and French colonel's shoulder boards. French camo trousers with reinforced knees are tucked into French combat boots. On his left hip he wears a Smith & Wesson .38 Special revolver.

# 75 'Colonel' Rolf Steiner

Rolf Steiner joined the French Foreign Legion in 1950 at the age of 17. He served in Indochina and then in Algeria where he took the parachute course at Blida and joined the 1st REP. After the abortive 'putsch' Steiner joined the OAS. He returned to France and tried civilian life for a few years, but soon tired of it. He was next hired by Biafra where he formed a commando unit to carry out special missions. After falling foul of a faction in Biafra and of the French SDECE Steiner left Biafra. Among the contracts he was offered after leaving Africa was one to lead a rescue mission for the imprisoned Tshombe. Steiner, however, next turned up in the South Sudan but left after about a year. He was handed over to the Sudanese government by the Ugandans and spent 3 years in a Sudanese prison before gaining his release and returning to Germany after more than 20 years away.

Steiner is illustrated in the uniform he wore while commanding the Commando Brigade in Biafra. He has retained his French Foreign Legion para's beret and beret badge. His camo utilities are also the 'lizard' pattern worn by French paras in Algeria. French paratrooper's boots and his French para's brevet complete the Gallic aspects of his uniform. On his right upper sleeve he wears the rising sun insignia of Biafra and the skull and crossbones insignia of the Commando Brigade.

# 76 Captain, Trucial Oman Scouts (c.1965)

Trucial Oman, not to be confused with the Sultanate of Muscat and Oman, consisted of what is now the United Arab Emirates. Between 1955 and 1970 defense for Trucial Oman was provided by the Trucial Oman Scouts, a well-trained and well-paid local force with British officers and NCOs. In addition to patrolling and thwarting Saudi Arabian attempts to snatch territory from Trucial Oman, the Scouts took part in the Jebel Akhdar campaign in conjunction with the Sultan's Armed Forces and the British 22nd Special Air Service Regiment.

The officer illustrated wears the TOS (Trucial Oman Scouts) red and white checkered 'kaffia' or 'schmarg' with a black 'agal', which, incidentally, was also used by the Bedouins to tie the feet of their camels while resting. The headdress badge for officers (as illustrated) bears crossed khunjah (daggers) while the enlisted badge bears only a single khunjah. The gray-blue shirt with British rank insignia – in this case three pips – on the shoulder loop and the red lanyard, khaki slacks, and red stable belt were the standard uniform of the TOS officer. Desert boots were highly favored foot gear. A khaki shirt was sometimes worn instead of the blue-gray one. When on patrol or in combat, this officer would be armed with a Browning 9 mm automatic pistol.

# 77 David Smiley, the Yemen (1960s)

David Smiley graduated from Sandhurst before World War II and served in the 1st Household Cavalry Regiment in Palestine. After the war began, however, Smiley began serving with various irregular units and was recruited into Special Operations Executive (SOE). He jumped into Greece and worked with Greek and, later, Albanian partisans. Towards the end of the war, he parachuted into Thailand and worked with irregulars there against the Japanese. During the late 1940s and early 1950s Smiley did a certain amount of conventional soldiering in Britain and Germany, but also served as military attaché in

Poland and Sweden. In 1958 he was offered the command of the Sultan of Muscat and Oman's armed forces, which he accepted. He held this command dur ng 1958–61, a period which included the Jebel Akhdar Campaign. After leaving the Sultan's service, Smiley was offered command of all three SAS regiments but chose to leave the Army instead. He was soon recruited for the Saudis, however, by an old SOE friend to act as an advisor to the royalist forces in the Yemen. Smiley later was given command of all of the mercenaries in the Yemen, including a small number of ex-SAS and a group of Frenchmen under Bob Denard.

As illustrated, Smiley is wearing traditional Yemeni attire. His white skull cap is known as a 'am-arraga'. Both his shirt and his 'iz-zar' (Yemeni skirt) are Khaki. Leather sandals complete his attire. His brown leather cartridge belt, holding Lee-Enfield stripper clips, is supported by crossed shoulder straps. Tucked into the belt he wears the large Yemeni-style jambiya. Note also, however, that behind it he has also tucked a Fairbairn-Sykes Commando dagger. The jambiya was intended as a defensive weapon, while the F-S was an offensive weapon, and it was standard Yemeni practice to carry a knife for each purpose. Smiley wears his watch on his wrist, though the Yemenis often strapped theirs to the jambiya. His rifle is a version of the Lee-Enfield, Mark I.

---

# 78 Islamic 'Volunteer', PLO Main Force, Lebanon (1983)

Within the ranks of the PLO are many Moslem volunteers from other countries (reportedly even including some American Black Muslims) and a few leftist soldiers of fortune of other faiths or no faith at all. For many of the Islamic volunteers, the PLO is fighting a 'Jihad' or holy war against Israel, and their involvement can be traced at least partially to the militarism of fundamentalist Islam. As a 'Main Force' member of one of the various PLO factions, this figure functions, in effect, as a professional soldier.

The traditional PLO headgear, the black and white 'shemagh', is worn over the shoulders around the neck, while a Libyan paratrooper's red beret with Libyan beret badge is worn. Since this 'fighter' also wears Libyan parachutist's wings on his left breast and since many Islamic soldiers or terrorists (depending on one's perspective) are trained in Libya, it is quite possible that this figure is a graduate of the parachute school at Ukba bin Naf'i. His camouflage jacket is in one of the patterns frequently worn by PLO 'elite' troops. In addition to the Libyan parachutist's wings – at least some of which were ordered for Libya by notorious ex-CIA agent Ed Wilson – he also wears a Syrian Commando badge on his right breast indicating further special training. Although complete camouflage uniforms are sometimes worn, this figure wears olive drab utility trousers, probably Syrian in origin. Tennis shoes are widely worn among PLO members, but Main Force fighters frequently wear black combat boots, with 'bug-out zippers' such as those shown. His magazine pouch is of a generic type very common to irregulars supplied by the Communist bloc and is one of the patterns widely used by the PLO. His weapon is the ubiquitous AKMS.

# 79 *William Baldwin, Kenya (1954)*

William Baldwin served in the US Navy from 1945–47 and attended the University of Colorado on the GI Bill, graduating in 1950. For the next three years he roamed the world working as a construction worker, commercial fisherman, roustabout;

whatever odd job he could find to feed himself and the 1953 BSA motorcycle he was riding during the later stages of his Odyssey. Ending up in Kenya, short of funds and in the midst of the Mau Mau uprising, Baldwin took the classic adventurer's route and joined the Kenya Police Reserve in June 1954. He served on counterterrorist operations with numbers 14 and 27 Platoons. After 13 months of seeing the terrorists' atrocities at close-quarters, Baldwin became a hardened terrorist-hunter who gave no quarter to an enemy who deserved none. Often, he put on 'black face' and African clothing to get close enough for the kill. After an American magazine interviewed Baldwin, who expressed his frank views about the desirability of killing Mau Maus, his visa was cancelled by the US government and he had to leave Kenya.

Baldwin wears the green beret of the Police Reserve and the 'jungle greens' normally worn in the bush on operations. The belt is the issue belt of the Police Reserve. His weapon is a Sterling submachine-gun, for which four spare magazines are carried in a canvas mag pouch on the left hip. Baldwin found the Sterling concealed reasonably well under the baggy coats worn by many Africans when he was working in 'black face'. Two No. 436 grenades are carried on the belt.

# 80 Bushman, 201 Battalion, South West African Territorial Force (1983)

The Bushmen were being systematically exterminated by SWAPO terrorists in Angola when South Africa allowed many of them to relocate in South West Africa. From these Bushmen 201 Battalion was formed. The battalion, which is divided into four rifle companies; two of which are normally in the bush on six week long operations, is used as a counterinsurgency force.

Because of the Bushmen's excellent tracking ability, their record for hunting down and killing terrorists is very good. The Bushmen make effective soldiers, though their rifle training takes a bit longer than normal since they have a tendency to aim high due to life-long use of the bow and arrow. On the other hand, their skill with the bow usually makes them effective with the 60 mm. light mortar.

The figure illustrated wears bush hat, shirt, trousers, and boots of South African pattern, though a khaki/brown beret bearing a beret badge with a black crow upon it may also be worn at times. His rifle is the FN. South African issue magazine pouches are worn on the pistol belt.

# 81 Major Mike Williams, Grey's Scouts, Rhodesia (1977)

Mike Williams served as an enlisted man with the 88th Infantry Division in Italy during World War II. After the war he was commissioned and in 1952 was assigned to the 10th Special Forces Group when it was activated. During the Korean War, he commanded a unit composed of North Korean and Chinese defectors. Until his discharge from the US Army in 1960, Williams continued to serve with Special Forces and airborne units.

In 1964 Williams went to Africa to fight in the Congo under Mike Hoare. In 1975 he returned to Africa and by 1976 he had received a captain's commission in the Rhodesian Army. When the protection company Williams was commanding was assigned a long section of railway to guard, Williams mounted his men on horseback. Williams not only had to train his troops – 'coloreds' of mixed parentage – to ride but also to shoot from horseback. After being promoted to major, Williams was transferred in July, 1977, to Rhodesia's famed mounted unit,

Grey's Scouts, as second in command. In February 1978, after about two years in the bush, Williams left Rhodesia, though reportedly his life has not been dull since then!

In the illustration, Williams wears the Rhodesian field or utility hat with the distinctive neck flap turned up. Cap, jacket, and trousers are all in the Rhodesian camouflage pattern. Rank slides are worn on the loops of the camo jacket. Boots are also standard Rhodesian Army issue items. In addition to the webbed belt only the chest pouch for rifle magazines is worn. This pouch, which was widely worn in Rhodesia, was especially useful for a horseman since it kept the pouches off the hips and thighs where they might be uncomfortable while mounted. His rifle, which has been painted in browns for camouflage, is the FN SLR.

# 82  Robert K. Brown

Robert K. Brown is a former officer in the US Army Special Forces, who upon leaving the Army became involved in free-lance soldiering. He is best-known as the publisher of *Soldier of Fortune* magazine but even after embarking upon a publishing career has remained a 'doer' who has sought adventure by aiding and advising (and occasionally going on combat operations with) anti-Communist forces in Rhodesia, Afghanistan, Guatemala, and El Salvador among other places. Recently, Brown has been part of a volunteer team of advisors working with elements of the Salvadoran Army.

Brown is portrayed as he was dressed for a foray into Afghanistan in 1982. To avoid arrest by Pakistani border guards, Brown dyed his mustache and hair black and donned Afghan turban, tunic, and trousers. The small fighting knife, webbed gear, and jungle boots are of US origin, however.

On an earlier trip to Darra on the Northwest Frontier of Pakistan, Brown, a weapons specialist in the Special Forces, had managed to obtain an example of the Soviet AK-74, which at that time was virtually unknown in the West, to examine and test fire. With much difficulty, Brown finally managed to arrange with one of Darra's arms merchants to test fire the AK-74, which had probably been taken from a dead Soviet airborne trooper in Afghanistan. The example brought for Brown's examination was missing its pistol grip, and this is the example of the AK-74 shown in Brown's hands.

# 83 *Mike Echanis*

Mike Echanis served in the US Army in Vietnam where he was seriously wounded. After recovering from his wounds, Echanis became a master at the martial art of Hwarang Do. He was later hired by the Department of Defense to train the US Navy SEALs, US Army Special Forces, and other such units in hand-to-hand combat, including the use of the blade.

In 1977, Echanis was hired by Nicaraguan President Somoza, whose son had been trained by Echanis at Fort Bragg. Echanis trained and led the Nicaraguan Anti-Terrorist Commandos and also advised and trained Somoza's bodyguards. Echanis's commandos proved to be the most effective fighting force in Nicaragua, but in September, 1978 he died in a plane crash into Lake Nicaragua.

Although Echanis's favorite 'uniform' consisted of black utilities, often worn with a black 'ninja' scarf or hood, photographs of him in Nicaragua show him wearing camo utilities, and this is how he is portrayed. A boonie hat much faded from the sun and sneakers complete his basic attire. Echanis's trademark weapon was the Gerber Mark II fighting knife, of which he often carried two. In this case he has one in his right hand and the tie-down for the sheath of the second one is visible on his left thigh. In a GI leather holster he carries a .45 automatic pistol.

---

# 84 *Mickey Marcus*

David 'Mickey' Marcus graduated from West Point in 1924. While serving in the Army, he attended law school at night. After resigning his commission, he worked at various civil service jobs, including Commissioner of Corrections for New York City. Marcus had retained a reserve commission upon leaving the Army, and in 1940 as war appeared likely he asked to return to active duty. With the rank of LTC he was assigned as judge advocate of the 27th Infantry Division.

Marcus was soon promoted to colonel, and after Pearl Harbor he commanded a jungle warfare school in Hawaii for a time. Marcus hoped for a combat command, but in 1943 he was assigned to the Pentagon. Though a 42-year-old staff officer who had never made a parachute jump, Marcus jumped with the 101st Airborne Division in Normandy. Marcus then fought alongside the paratroopers until his superior officer in Washington learned of his whereabouts and ordered him back to the States. At the end of the war Marcus was involved in setting up the military government for Germany and in the Nüremberg war crimes trials.

Marcus left the Army in spring, 1947, but at the end of that year was contacted by representatives of the soon-to-be-born state of Israel and asked to come to Palestine to act as a military advisor. Though he was a Jew, Marcus had not considered himself a Zionist. Still, he agreed to go.

Marcus's greatest contribution was in helping to organize

the Jewish state's fighting forces and in training them. Marcus helped write the training manuals and organize an army staff. He also used his West Point training to evaluate the most likely invasion routes the Arabs would choose.

Under the nom de guerre 'Brigadier General Stone', Marcus was given command in the 1948 Arab–Israeli War of the Jerusalem Front, where he helped break through to the surrounded Jewish enclave in the city. Shortly before the ceasefire ending the 1948 War went into effect, Marcus was accidentally killed by one of his own sentries.

Marcus wears a khaki shirt and OD shorts. The latter started out as trousers but became 'field expedient' shorts after an Egyptian Spitfire had strafed them while they were hanging on the line. Marcus cut the bullet-riddled legs off and created these shorts. His footwear is World War II US military issue combat boots. In his left hand he carries one of the home-workshop Stens manufactured in Palestine before independence. Also barely visible on his left hand is his West Point class ring, which Marcus wore proudly while in Palestine.

## 85 Legionnaire of Special Operations Unit (c.1978)

The SOE ('Seccion de Operaciones Especiales') is the Legion unit which is specially trained to carry out reconnaissance and raiding missions. The figure illustrated is dressed for a night raiding mission. Although he does not wear any headgear, the green scarf around his neck could be wrapped around his head if so desired. Camouflage has been applied to his face. His shirt is the standard Legion light green one, but with olive green sweater worn over it. The four-pocket (two on each side) green utility trousers are worn bloused into issue black combat boots. On his webbed belt he wears a 'cuchillo' (a heavy-bladed fighting knife) and a double magazine pouch for 40-round magazines for his Star Z-62 SMG. Note that in his left hand he holds two 30 round magazines for this weapon which have been taped together so that a fast change can be made by just reversing them.

## 86 *Corporal, Armored Cavalry, 'Grupos Ligeros Saharianos II' (c.1976)*

Legion armored cavalry units have been equipped with US M41 light tanks, French AMX-13 light tanks, French AML-90 light armored cars, and French Panhard M-3 APCs. Each armored cavalry battalion provides support for one of the Tercios.

The figure illustrated wears armored crewman's helmet with sand goggles and the blue two-piece armored crew uniform. Note that Legion insignia is still worn on the shoulder loops and that corporal's insignia is worn on the left breast. The trousers bear four side pockets in the same pattern as those on the standard green utilities and are gathered at the ankles. As with many Legion units in the Sahara, sandals are worn rather than boots. The only thing worn on the webbed gear is the holster for the Super Star 9 mm. pistol, which the figure is firing.

## 87 *Legionnaire, Sahara (c.1975)*

The Legionnaire illustrated wears the 'siroquera' over his green utility hat. This camouflage 'siroquera' and the camouflage utilities being worn were adopted in 1975 shortly before the Legion left the Sahara early in 1976. In November, 1975, 250,000–350,000 Moroccans had taken part in King Hassen's 'March of Conquest' but had stopped short of forcing a confrontation with the Legion. A negotiated settlement was reached, however, and the Legionnaires were pulled out of the Sahara, though a Legion presence remained in North Africa at Ceuta and Melilla.

Sand goggles are worn over the 'siroquera'. Note also that the utility hat is equipped with a chin strap, a useful feature in a sandstorm. A black scarf is worn around the neck. The belt carries magazine pouches for 20 round CETME magazines. His weapon is the CETME M58 assault rifle.

## 88 Portuguese Mercenary, Angola (1976)

White mercenaries fought with both the FNLA (Frente Nacional de Libertacao de Angola) and UNITA (Uniao de Nacional para a Independencia Total de Angola) during the Angolan Civil War. In fact, some white mercenaries were either executed or imprisoned after the MPLA (Movimento Popular de Libertacao de Angola) victory. Although some of the American and British mercenaries in Angola have probably received more publicity, Portuguese mercenaries were among the most effective, many having fought in Angola previously with the Portuguese Army. A few of these Portuguese soldiers of fortune continue fighting with UNITA in a guerrilla war against the Marxist government of Angola today.

The Portuguese mercenary illustrated appears to be a former member of the Portuguese airborne forces (which are assigned to the Air Force) since he wears their green beret and parachutist's wings. Portuguese camouflage utilities and combat boots are also worn. The shoulder slide in black indicates colonial service and carries the single chevron of a lance corporal. On the webbed belt he has a magazine pouch for extra rifle magazines with US M26 'frags' affixed to it. The weapon is noteworthy, being the Armalite AR-10, a 7.62 mm. NATO caliber predecessor to the M-16 which was issued in limited number to Portuguese personnel.

## 89 Swiss Guardsman, the Vatican (1983)

The current Swiss Guard consists of 100 men, including four officers, five senior NCOs, and eighteen junior NCOs. All recruits must be Swiss, Catholic, unmarried, and at least 5 feet 9 inches tall. Recruits must also have completed basic military training in Switzerland. Upon joining the Swiss Guard, 15 days of basic training with the halberd is undergone.

The figure illustrated is on duty outside the Papal apartments and wears the traditional blue, red, and yellow Renaissance-style uniform. The traditional halberd and sword are carried, but in response to a possible threat on the Pontiff's life he is drawing the Beretta M12 SMG kept concealed in an umbrella stand for such emergencies.

## 90 American 'Security Advisor', Guatemala (1983)

Because of the guerrilla war going on in Guatemala, outlying ranches find it necessary to maintain their own security forces, and some American soldiers of fortune have been recruited to train and lead these para-military units.

The Figure illustrated wears a US OD utility hat with RANGER and AIRBORNE arcs, 5th SFG(A) flash, and Selous Scouts beret badge, the combination indicating rather impressive military credentials. The utilities are Guatemalan Army pattern worn with US jungle boots. A pistol belt carries a Colt .38 Super caliber auto on the right hip and spare magazines on the left hip. A cartridge belt for buckshot rounds is also worn. The long gun is a Benelli Police/Military semi-auto assault shotgun.

# 91 *Caporal, 1st REC (c.1978)*

The 1st REC (Régiment Étrangère de Cavalerie) is composed of 800 men and since 1967 has been stationed at Orange in France where it can provide security for strategic nuclear installations and airfields. The three armored car squadrons of the 1st REC are equipped with Panhard AML-90 armored cars and would serve as the armored reconnaissance regiment for the 14th Infantry Division if at war. The 1st REC is also a part of France's intervention force 'Guepard' and as such has seen action in Chad within the last few years.

The corporal illustrated wears the standard green fibre armored crewman's helmet with earphone shells and wire boom microphone. Either the Legion green beret or white képi is worn by members of the 1st REC for parades or other duties, however. Although the M1964 green utilities tailored in Legion fashion are standard for members of the 1st REC, this figure apparently wears a coverall of the type often used by armored crewmen. His boots are standard black combat boots. In the center of his chest he wears a plastic junction box for the microphone and earphone jacks. Just below this junction box, affixed with velcro, is his rank insignia.

His weapon is the MAT49 SMG, the standard issue weapon for armored crewmen, though the vehicle commander normally carries a pistol.

---

## 92 Caporal, 2nd Cie, 2nd REP (c.1983)

The 2nd REP (Régiment Étrangère de Parachutistes) is the inheritor of the Legion's para tradition and is today stationed at Calvi, Corsica. The 650 men of the 2nd REP are part of the French 11th Parachute Division and are often used as France's premier intervention force, as at Kolwezi on 19–20 May 1978 when the 2nd REP made their most recent combat jump. Members of the 2nd REP have also seen action in Chad and been used as 'peace-keepers' in the Lebanon. Each company of the 2nd REP is especially trained for special operations as follows: 1st – night operations and anti-tank; 2nd – mountain and ski operations; 3rd – amphibious operations; 4th – demolitions, sabotage, and sniping.

The figure illustrated wears the Legion green beret with parachutist's beret badge. Note that this beret badge is the old Metropolitan para beret badge, which is today worn only by the Legion paras. Other Legion regiments wear the same beret but wear the Legion grenade as their beret badge. The green leather 'mountain' jacket is worn by members of the 2nd Company. Rank insignia is worn on the shoulder boards, Legion 'écusson' on the upper left sleeve, name tag on the left breast, parachutist's brevet on the right breast, and company crest on the right pocket fob. A green turtleneck sweater is worn beneath the jacket. Closely-tailored M1964 green utility trousers are tucked into French paratrooper's boots (in this case Soules which are roughly equivalent to American Corcorans).

# 93 Legionnaire, 13th DBLE, Djibouti (c.1977)

The 13th DBLE (Demi-Brigade de la Légion Étrangère) has been in Djibouti since leaving Algeria in 1962. When Djibouti became independent in 1977, the 13th DBLE remained as part of the French garrison. Legionnaires in Djibouti are at Camp de Gabode (the HQ of the 13th DBLE), Obock, Holl-Holl, and Queah. The four combat companies of the 13th DBLE are motorized and carry out reconnaissance patrols along Djibouti's borders.

The Legionnaire illustrated wears the one-piece, all-white képi many Legionnaires purchase in lieu of using the traditional white képi cover. Because he is stationed in the tropics, this Legionnaire wears a khaki drill, short-sleeved shirt and shorts with a matching webbed belt. Long white socks and black dress shoes complete the uniform. On the shirt are worn the regimental crest on the right pocket fob, fourragère at the left shoulder, and shoulder boards.

# 94 Rifleman, 1/7 Duke of Edinburgh's Own Gurkha Rifles, (Falklands War)

A total of 750 men of the 1/7 Duke of Edinburgh's Own Gurkha Rifles saw action in the South Atlantic War as part of 5 Brigade. Actually, the Gurkhas did not really get a chance to see much action, but they were a potent psychological weapon, since the Argentines seemed to believe their own propaganda about 'head-hunting mercenaries', and the fear of kukri-armed Gurkhas no doubt influenced many Argentine soldiers to surrender.

The Gurkhas took over responsibility for Goose Green from the 2nd Battalion, the Parachute Regiment, who had carried out the assault on Argentine defenders at that settlement. After the Paras left, the Gurkhas completed the mopping up operations in that area. The Gurkhas also took part in the battle for the high ground around Port Stanley.

The Gurkha illustrated wears the heavy CW (Cold Weather) cap and the CW Parka and trousers – all in DPM camouflage pattern – over quilted liners. Note that a wooley-pulley sweater and a shirt are also worn beneath the jacket. 'Boots, DMS' are worn with puttees. His weapon is the L1A1 SLR.

## 95 *Piper, 7th Duke of Edinburgh's Own Gurkha Rifles (c.1971)*

There has always been a certain affinity between the Scottish Highlanders and the Gurkhas dating back to the many battles these highlanders from two parts of the world fought together in India. As a result, the pipes are an honored tradition in the Gurkha regiments, and many Gurkha pipers are graduates of the Army School of Bagpiping at Edinburgh Castle. Gurkha pipes and drums are usually a big hit when they perform, too. When the 1/7th visited the US Army's Rangers at Ft Lewis, Washington, in 1983, for example, their pipes and drums were a special attraction.

The piper illustrated wears the standard pillbox hat with cap badge of the 7th Gurkha Rifles. The white full dress patrol jacket is worn over green trousers. White gaiters cover the shoes. The pipe banner, presented by the Duke of Edinburgh, bears the Duke's coat of arms on one side and the regimental badge and battle honors on the obverse. Plaid, bag, and ribbons are in Douglas tartan.

# 96 Sergeant Rambahadur Limbu, VC, 10th Princess Mary's Own Gurkha Rifles

Then Lance Corporal Rambahadur Limbu won his VC in Sarawak during November, 1965, and has remained the only holder of the Victoria Cross serving on active duty in the British Army today. Now a captain, Rambahadur Limbu was named one of the Queen's Gurkha Orderly Officers in 1983.

In this illustration, the traditional Gurkha pillbox hat is worn with the cap badge of the 10th Gurkha Rifles. The uniform is the No. 2 dress with regimental lanyard and shoulder loop insignia. His belt buckle also bears the unit crest. Most noteworthy amongst the medals worn is, of course, the Victoria Cross.